YOU ARE THE CONQUEROR

DR. PRATIBHA V. DAVE

INDIA • SINGAPORE • MALAYSIA

Dedication

Dedicated to my

Revered Guruji
Param Pujya Swami Parmatmanandji Saraswati.
Convener of "Acharya Sabha"

Contents

The Book

This book is a treat of Vedantic Vision about how to live intelligently. Happy and successful life devoid of stress.

वेदांतो नाम उपनिषद् प्रमाणम्।

Vedanto naam upanishd pramaanam"

(words are the means of knowledge). Only by words of Upanishads this knowledge of self can be gained.

Upnishad – word is derived from Sanskrit Dhatu "Sad" (सद्) – "Sad" means "to destroy" or "to loosen" or "to reach". "Up" (उप) means near. So – to reach which is near. Who is the most near to me? So many objects – Pen, chair, book, watch, my cloths etc. But the most near to me is "I". "I" is nearest to me but I have forgotten "I" – (Consciousness – Atma).

Ni (नि) – means well ascertained. Therefore, Upanishad means "knowledge of "I" – who is nearest to me. And for well ascertained knowledge of who am "I"? – I will have to study Upnishad from a capable teacher – who knows methodology of teaching Upnishads.

ॐ is the sweetest name of Ishwara (God). It is a sound symbol – which transcends all the three states of our life. Waking, dream and is deep sleep (Sushupti) and sustains them.

Everyone wants to be happy, secure and complete and wants to live one day more happily without being ignorant. Human being is self-conscious and endowed with the free will. This-endowments make man-kind to improve and be different. Because self-consciousness – human being Judges – about him/herself and concludes. "I am small, unhappy, inadequate" – and whole life spent in changing/improving him/herself and the world around. This creates tremendous pressure – but by putting any number of efforts and accomplishing in many spheres – the persistent sense of "lacking something" doesn't go away. Then circumstances are blamed and from the depth of heart one cries "Why me?". This is not a personal problem – it is Universal.

If you analyse, you can see that – the main reason of sorrows and afflictions faced are due to hurts and guilts, stressful life and sense of "lacking Something" – resulting to notions of being limited, insignificant and unsuccessful. This also is a Universal Problem.

Bhagvad Geeta and Upnishads address these basic human problems and point out permanent solutions (not patchwork) for those basic problems of human kind.

All can't have easy approach to Upnishads. Bhagvad – Geeta. Swami Vivekanand said "Bhagvad Geeta is a bouquet – composed of beautiful flowers of spiritual truth collected from Upnishads". Bhagvad Geeta is not a religious message, it is for humanity to live an intelligent and Successful human life. It can be asked that – "Can the message given before 5000 years – be relevant and useful now – in our day to day life?" The answer is "YES". Because of two reasons. Firstly Geeta talks about "Truth" – and truth can never be negated. Truth is changeless for ever. Secondly – Geeta addresses basic problems of human – kind – which are universal and persist irrelevant of time and place. Besides – Bhagvad Geeta re-introduces you with your self.

Bhagvad Geeta's main message is "मा शुच: ।" "don't be sorrowful – ever". It doesn't talk about absence of sorrows but shows – there is no any cause for sorrow what so ever.

This book focuses on the problems – which we are facing in our day to day life – we face manyfold afflictions and terrified by tiger of ego. We are roaming around in forest of birth, old age diseases and death. Geeta Proclaims, "Be not Weak – Be fearless" and recommends Karmyoga – which in time leads to clarity of mind & purity of living.

Bhagvad Geeta points out actions with right attitude – Karmyoga – to exhaust mental weakness and dirt. Karmyoga prepares mind to face any situation in right way – While it maintains inner content and composure. Therefore, this knowledge is for everyone – anywhere at any stage, at any age, especially for children and youths.

This book also attempts to unfold the beauty and subtlety of the message of Bhagvad Geeta and Upanishad's in the conflicts and restlessness in lack of inner composure of modern world. Therefore, go through this Vedantic treat and

- Conquest your stress.
- Conquest your hurts & guilts.
- Smartly and wisely relate with the world with an attitude and win it.
- Be brave, fearless and immortal.
- Follow – These 10 golden success – rules from Bhagvad Geeta –
  And
- Know you are the Conqueror – Now.

*****

The Author

Dr. Pratibha Dave is a voluntarily retired – Civil Surgeon and Chief District Medical Officer. It was her dream from her childhood to become a doctor, not with a view to pursue a lucrative practice yielding lot of money, prestige and fame but Just to Serve the humankind – particularly for deprived and suffering section of this country.

She worked as a Class – II medical officer, then as Anaesthesiologist / Superintendent – Class – I Officer and then as Civil – Surgeon / CDMO.

When she was working as medical officer in a civil hospital – she witnessed unusually large number of – "avoidable looking." deaths on operation tables. Which she presumed– may be – because of lack of expertise in process & procedures of anaesthetising patients.

So, she took leave without pay – and opted for Anaesthesiology as her specialisation – At that time there was not any Qualified Anaesthesiologist in any of the Civil Hospitals of the district. She did her M.D. – returned to the Civil Hospital – where she worked as a medical officer – and not only worked ceaselessly to ameliorate and save operative patients from pain, other complications and fatal outcome, but spent a substantial portion of her earnings to help the poor in meeting with expenses of costly medicines and nutrition.

Such a righteous life invariably leads to spirituality in the deepest and truest sense of the term, Thus, she was attracted to study of Vedanta from competent Acharyas. Such as Swami Dayanandji Maharaj, Swami Parmatmanandji Saraswati and Swami Shbodhanandji Saraswati of Siddhabari – led her to retire early for full time pursuing of Vedanta – Study. She rigorously studied Vedantic texts in depth by attending regular Vedanta Classes, short and long term residential retreats at Rishikesh – Dayanda Ashram, Coimbatore – Anaikatti – Arsh Vidya Gurukulam in down south and siddhbari in Himalayas. Now she regularly teaches Vedanta through social media. She wrote well received series of articles on Vedanta and stress management in IMA magazine (Rajkot), the Gujarati version of which was published in "Arsha Vidya Darshan." She also wrote series of articles on "Relating to the world is Relating to the Ishwara" in Arsha Vidya Darshan. She wrote a book (novel – in Gujarati) – taking seeds from her own experiences of working in her medical field – named "Saundarya nu Ganu Mukhe Mare hajo" – (Let there be song of beauty on my lips = in any circumstances) published by "Pravin Prakashan" and by "Blue rose Publishers" – as named "Dr. Vibha."

This book of hers – contains valuable practical guidance to true happiness, real tranquillity and basic equilibrium in the prevailing chaos of this troubled modern world – based upon our ancient wisdom of Bhagvad Geeta and Upnishads. As Swami Vivekanand has said all other philosophical systems and religions are Just distant echoes of what Vedanta stands for. She is confident this book will introduce the sincere readers to this wonderful world of true inner happiness, composure and fulfilment.

*****

Chapter 1

Grow Over Your Stress

Invite Ananda and Peace into your mind and allow to rest into your heart. Smoothly unload your heart from everything else. Put aside all your complaints and make place for harmony. Be loving and compassionate to all beings and yourself. close your eyes slowly – the upper lid touching the lower – smoothly and connect with Ishwara – immerse yourself into Prarthana (Prayer) without asking anything. Just be with Ishwara.

The word "stress" and its experience are not new to anyone.

The stress and strain have a direct relation to the basic and universal problem of human being who is endowed with "free will" – and so wants to be different, wants to improve and because of self-consciousness human being has self – consciousness and because of that has self-judgement, and because of self-judgement has complexes. The life of becoming, the attempts of improving and being different create tremendous pressure on one's mind and this pressure results in "Stress and Strain".

Which are the areas – the stress and strain comes from? Does it come from without or within? Has it any advantages? What's about coping abilities and coping techniques? These are the key questions about the stress and strain.

To tackle this stress many remedies have been advocated -but almost all prove to be a patchwork! Unless the root of the problem is not understood – how any problem can be tackled successfully? The scriptures – the body of knowledge Vedas – and Upanishads (Vedanta) address this problem right at its roots and offer it's sure solution. If the knowledge is assimilated – one can live a life free from stress and strain.

What is scripture?

The scriptures – has four components. [a] Shruti, [b] Smruti, [c] Puran and [d] History.

Among these four components Sruti addresses the basic problems of human beings which are of feeling limited, inadequate, incomplete and insecure. After all efforts to become constantly happy and complete and achieving so many accomplishments – he/she doesn't become free from the sense of inadequacy and insecurity. Then a thought may sprout out – that – may – be there is no connection between what he/she does and what he/she wants! And the quest "to know" starts! "When the absence of connection between what one wants and what one does" is seen the seer is the VIVEKI [the discriminative person]. The – section "Jnanakand" is for such VIVEKI. Shruti (श्रुति) is not product of human mind. Its subject matter is beyond our sense organs. Shruti is Truth and so changeless. It addresses our basic problems – problem of sense of limitation and inadequacy. Shruti gives knowledge of true nature of self – Atma (consciousness). Assimilation of this knowledge gives freedom from the sense of – inadequacy, insecurity and unhappiness. The Smruti – like Yajnavalkya Smruti, Manusmruti etc. are like our constitution – according to the need of the time – place and culture of the society – it changes. There are 18 Puran-s like "Shiva puran" "Vishnu puran" etc. This section tells stories of conspicuous role models in alignment of Shruti. If studied – one can have his/her role model to admire and follow. And Ramayan, Mahabharat are histories.

There are four VEDAS – 1. Rigveda, 2. Yajurveda, 3. Samveda and 4. Atharvaveda. Vedas talk about Karma (action-s) and Dharma (duties). The definition of Dharma is "To do right in any given – situation". Vedas also talk about common duties which are universal – and – duties to be performed as per roles played as a father mother, sibling etc. Vedas also talk about **1.** Duties to be performed daily. **2.** Duties and rituals to be performed on special occasions like birth, death, completing 60 years (Shashthipoorti) etc.**3.** Actions performed to fulfil desires. (काम्यकर्म-s) Vedas talk about means and ends also. This is Action session and it's big one. There is another section which is for eligible – those who are eager to know (true nature of self) and want freedom from sorrows, afflictions and unhappiness for ever. These are the persons who have realized very clearly that after living a life of becoming after endless worldly accomplishments, after all efforts to become happy – they do not come out of sense of inadequacy, they want to be happy and complete – but all efforts for the same – leave them still inadequate and unhappy. Then even in sleep and at the moment of joy they do become happy in spite of presence of all their problems as they are. What can be this? May be – there is no connection between what they do and what they want? May be – their conclusion about themselves that they are limited, inadequate, incomplete – is wrong? And the quest "to know" starts! When the absence of connection between what one wants and what one does is seen – the seer is a discriminative person. The section of knowledge is for such discriminative one.

Vedanta addresses these basic problems of human being. As this knowledge obtains at the end of Veda it is called Vedanta. Some Vedanta sections are there in the midst of Vedas. The meaning of word **"Antah"** (अंतः) is – well determined final decision – also. Therefore – Vedanta also means that – do anything, accomplish everything but If you want to become happy and complete, want fullness – you need to know your intrinsic nature – self and that's final – a well determined fact. So "ANTAH" means the final decision. Vedanta is final decision of VEDA'S.

Human being is self-conscious and endowed with freedom of desiring and using faculties as wished. The lives and abilities of animals are programmed. While human being is free regarding actions. He/she can perform an action, may not perform or perform the same in different way. That's very important. At the same time – this freedom has an element of pressure which comes from self-consciousness. Because of the complete self-consciousness – there is self-judgement which results in complexes and therefore problems too. Animals have no complexes and so – no problems too. Animals don't want to be different or wants to improve. This feeling of being different and to improve of human being is not personal – it is universal.

The psychological problems vary from person to person but everybody wants to be uninterruptedly happy and secure, no one wants to die and can't tolerate being ignorant. Everyone wants and needs approval of oneself and world around. And in his/ her attempts to become happy and complete human wants to change him/her self and the world. Human being is given free will – therefore he/she may perform – any particular action – may not perform the same or perform it differently. If this free will is rightly and discriminatively used one's life can become smoother and free from conflicts. Besides every human being knows without being taught that – what is right and what's wrong. What one wants from others for him/her self – i.e. – Respect, good conduct, discipline, no lying, no stealing, no killing etc. – are the same things others want from him/her self. Therefore, man or woman, child and adults, educated and no educated – all know what is right and wrong. Then even in attempt of improving and being different– we suffer tremendous pressure forcing us to transgress Dharma (to do right in any given situation) which creates lots of stress and strain on our minds. The struggle of becoming causes – anxiety, worry, tension, pressure, disappointment, conflicts – failures, demands, targets, agony, – causing a constant disturbance on an individual's mind and results in stress and strain. In long run this condition gives rise to – cardiac, mental, central nervous system and digestive system's diseases. Areas from where stress can come.ss

1. Individual level,
2. Family level,
3. Work situations,
4. Environmental factor,
5. Feeling of lack of love and appreciation.

(1) Individual Level

At individual level stress comes – from.

1. Goals.
2. Motivation.
3. Excess of "I ness" – and
4. Incompetency.

- **Goals:** I should fix my goals with great discrimination and should be very clear – about – my abilities. My goals must be realistic. Once I fix my goals – there should be clear cut priorities. If this is not done there will be confusion in my mind causing tension and stress.

- **Motivation:** If my goals are totally selfish – they create tension. Unfortunately, many use the method of manipulation and this pull and push approach is very tiring and produces exhaustion and stress.
- **Incompetency:** To cope with the goals – I have fixed – I must have skill and abilities. If I am not competent enough to achieve the goals it will create stress in my mind.
- **Excess of "I ness":** Actually – this is identification with – BMS complex. (Body, mind, senses assembly.) This produces much stress. Actually, stress is in proportion of degree and intensity of your identification with BMS complex. Vedanta beautifully explains– how? And shows cognitive solution.

When I say "This is my pen" "This is my car" "This is my son" and so on… then I clearly know that the pen, car, son are not "I". The things I can objectify – can't be me. In this world there are two things – I and everything else. Everything else is object of my objectification and I am the one who objectify. I am the knower and all other objects are known and objects of my knowledge are always different from me. But confusion starts when this comes to myself! I say "My finger" "My eyes" "I am tall" etc. – I am talking about my body. When I say "I am hungry – thirsty" I am talking about my प्राण:– meaning my physiology. When I say "Leave me alone – I am in bad mood" – I am talking about my mind. I say "I took this decision "I talk about my intellect – that part of my mind which takes decisions.

(Actually, this is called Anth Karan having four types of functions] **(a)** Mind which is responsible for fancies, desires, doubts. **(b)** Intelligence-analysis, taking decisions, knowing – any knowledge pertaining to this world in any field and Adhyatmic (knowledge about true nature of oneself, creation, consciousness, jiva and God – and their interconnection) all take place here only. **(c)** chit – where the knowledge one gathers is stored – memories. **(d)** Ego – this ego is not that in which one thinks "I am the best – supreme" and consider others insignificant but this is continuous awareness about "I". Everyone knows that "I am" without using any means of knowledge. ss

Here also I objectify my body, mind, physiology and intellect then how can I be the things I objectify? But here there is confusion because of identification with my body mind senses complex. I superimpose my body mind senses complex upon the "I". Two objects of opposite nature can't mix as milk and water will mix as both have similar nature but milk and some pieces of iron will not mix having opposite nature. Here "I" and all other objects are having opposite nature "I" is consciousness while all other objects of the world including my BMS complex – are inert – how they can mix being totally different in their nature? But see, here they mix up intimately! There – some strange thing happened which is actually not possible but this has happened! This is called by Vedanta– Adhyas – meaning mistake in recognizing. Not recognizing what is actually there. For example – if you put behind a crystal ball a red flower – then that colourless crystal ball picks up the red colour of the flower and looks red. Actually, – it is as it was – colourless – but looks red coloured. Similarly the BMS complex because of proximity – takes the attributes of Consciousness – Atma (consciousness) and the inert BMS complex seems to be – Consciousness. And I superimpose my body, mind, sense complex upon the "I".

Besides, I play many roles in my life and except in a state of deep sleep – I constantly relate to the world. It seems that with a change in the object I am relate with – there is relevant change in "I". If the object is son – I become a father or a mother. If the object is my father I become a son or daughter. I like an object – I become a liker. If I dislike – a thing I turn into disliker. But when I say – "I am father" "I am daughter" "I am seer" "I am listener" etc. "I am" is involved in each. "I am" is invariable – while variable is father, son, seer, listener etc. Therefore, the father is me but "I" is not the father, son is me but "I" is not the son. There is "I" in the father, there is "I" in the son – but the "I" is free from the both. But there is every possibility of my taking myself as a role – if the invariable "I" is not clear to me.

Suppose – a well – known and popular film actor plays a role of a rich man turned into bagger – a mountain of sorrows because -of unfortunate events fell upon him. He acts the role superbly and can shed real tears – and makes the audience also cry. But while shedding tears he congratulates himself and pleased inside for being able to do so.

In the film the role of bagger has problems causing him unhappiness which leads to shedding tears. There is no any physical distance between the actor and the bagger. But in spite of bagger's problems, the actor remains unaffected and free from the problems of the role – the bagger. The bagger's physical body entirely depends on the actor's body and the bagger is definitely that actor and if that is so – then the bagger's problems should also be actor's problem too – but that is not the case. Even though the bagger is the actor – the actor is not the bagger. There is difference between bagger and the actor but not physical distance. In the sense of actor's knowledge he – the actor is not the role – bagger. The actor knows that the bagger is the assumed role. Actor remembers himself as a popular, very rich actor and plays the role of bagger according to the script. Similarly, he can play many and any roles without losing himself regardless whether script is pleasant or unpleasant.

Suppose, now, that if the actor forgets himself while playing the role of bagger and when villain slaps him and the role bagger and the role bagger is to speak an emotional dialogue but actor forgets the script and following the slap gets so angry that he strikes back! The director has to pull the curtain down and ask, "Hey, what's the matter?"

"He slapped me hard. Do you think I am going to let him get away with that?"

And telling this he again hits the villain right there. What is the problem? The actor's problem is confusion between himself and his role. There is no action on the part of the actor now but reaction. Actor is no more an actor but a reactor because he has no self-awareness. There is no role playing on his part.

Now, in life you play many different roles as father, son, citizen, employer, employee, husband, wife …and if you have a problem as father, son, daughter, husband or wife – you must know that there is confusion between yourself and the role. When "I" totally identifies with the role of father, son, husband, wife etc. along with the reacting mind then "I" suffers the reaction of mind. However, the role is no doubt the "I" – I am definitely not the role. If you have problems as a father, son or husband – then you are not playing the role, you have become the role – just like that actor who forgetting his identity – strikes back to villain. You will not act but react suffering all the sorrows of the roles you are playing. Therefore, if you play your roles without losing yourself to the roles – you will act and not react. This attitude and understanding can solve most of your problems. And this understanding just remove the false identification – the "I-ness-ego."

(2) The second factor from which stress comes is from Family level.
Stress can come from
1.   Financial problem if any.
2.   Degree of responsibilities and
3.   Relations in-between family members.

Financial Problems

This can be of two types. Firstly – lack of enough money, secondly – Too much money. Vedanta says – there is nothing wrong in earning money or to earn much money is wrong. Money has it's own value and everybody should respect it. The wealth has been worshipped in Bhartiya culture as Goddess Lakshmi. But the pressure of earning and collecting money should not be such that it forces you to transgress Dharma (that is to do right in any given situation). Here it's to be taken in consideration that Vedanta does not admit "good and bad" – it admits only "right and wrong" and everybody knows – without being taught – what is right and what is wrong. It is well known that too much money brings many faults and defects with it because such wealth is always earned snatching rights of others or by causing suffering to others.

Degree of responsibilities in family. Naturally – if there is an old bed – ridden member to look after or a physically or mentally challenged child – that will cause an extra tension.

If there are strained relations in-between family members – between father–son, husband-wife, mother-daughter will definitely add to one's tension and stress.

Now, look at the point – my body, mind, intellect, parentage, relations, friends, circumstances, birth place, memory, job – all "is given" to me and I have to take what is given! I need to have an attitude which is appropriate to reality. And everything is put together intelligently – my eyes to see, ears to hear, hands with their fingers having tips and joints, stomach, liver, kidneys, brain and everything. If I analyse the scheme of things which hold a certain order – I can see – what is there? Which I exactly produce at my own will and efforts? Laws like the law of Gravitation, Oxygen, carbon dioxide, sun, moon, light and heat, means and ends – all are given. This earth rotates round on its middle vertical axis and it's a little tilt are given. Not only my parentage – but after birth my capacity to grow into adult and subjected to old age and the death is given. Plants and trees and the balance of oxygen and other gases, time and space, memory and the means and ends are given. Possibility of collapse is also given. Stars and galaxies may be born and die away. One organism no more and an another may be in the making – these all within order.

Human genius – intelligence is given – therefore human being can invent but I cannot say "I am author of this or that." I understand because I am given the faculty of understanding. Even though I make some big invention and the society adores me – I can-not say myself being the author! – but I can be objective and see that "Everything is given". and all have been put together intelligently to serve a purpose. In this world nothing new can be created. The word "Discovery" is spiritual! By using it we humbly accept – it was there – but was covered. Covered with our ignorance – now – it is discovered. Therefore, we have no chance of choice. There is one beautiful prayer.

"O Lord, may I have the maturity to accept totally – gracefully, what I can't change, the will and efforts to change what I can and the knowledge of the difference between what I can and can't change."

So – first you will have to accept – Accept yourself, accept the world around and accept your circumstances. After showing the maturity of graceful acceptance – you can do many things. You can change your attitude towards yourself and the world around, you can tighten up your personal life if it is loose, if it is too tight – you can loosen up, you can repair any damage done. Accept that you can-not alter what has happened. Don't victimized you by regret, sadness, anger, agitation on this score. Accept the past as it is. All that happened may be valid for you to be what you are today. Actually, what we are now – is prescribed by us only – with our past actions.

Let there be no confusion between "you" and your "roles". Act – do not react.

Perform your duties with Yajna spirit. (यज्ञ) is a ritual with different sacrifices – in form of ghee and other holy materials – are offered to fire in a particularly shaped "Yajnakund" with chanting particular mantras for welfare of the people or to fulfil certain desires. Every Yajna involves sacrifices – and as in performing own duties – and sometimes not easy to perform kind – involve some kind of sacrifice and so this act of performing duties when performed – is also considered as (Yajna) Duty demands – small or big – sacrifice. To bring up a child is duty of it's parents. Though it gives tremendous joy – the process also demands lots of sacrifices. Is that not true? To top in a tough examination, to perform challenging job like– of a doctor, manager, administrator, mountaineer, house – wife, prime minister etc. Duties of all demand sacrifice. Without sacrifice no duty can be performed. Vedanta states that performing duties only can give one purification and subtlety of mind. Duties are considered worship. When duties are performed – whether it is easy or hard, convenient or inconvenient – because it's my duty I will perform-with that attitude – in this changed spirit – it gives tremendous joy and satisfaction.

(3) The third factor from which stress comes is

Work Situation

If you work in a field you have chosen – you like it very much – you enjoy your work. If you have to work which you don't like it causes tiredness and boredom and you, then complain against you, your parents, your circumstances and the system – you don't have job-satisfaction.

At work place you may face interference, overwork, idiot boss, unhealthy atmosphere, lack of proper staff and all these add to your stress. One doesn't get always job or field of work – according to one's choice, liking and skill. It may happen – that you wanted to become a singer but because of your father's insistence you had to go for medical profession. You are famous and a successful practitioner – then even you have dissatisfaction at the same time. And it is also a fact that any work – how much liked and challenging – in long run it becomes monotonous and produces boredom.

Therefore better – you like your job-whatever it is. Every work – small or big Vedanta – considers it – as spiritual endeavour or rites. It is the means by which you can neutralize your strong likes and dislikes – which in turn gives you purity of mind and – clarity in life. The job is your duty and performing it nicely and honestly – without complaining – with interest makes one innovative. This attitude of "Yajna Spirit" relieves you from much stress and negative effects of likes and dislikes. So, you accept your field of work gracefully and work with interest – considering it as your duty – your Dharma – i.e. – doing right in the given situation.

(4) The fourth factor from which stress comes is environmental factors. – pollution, noises, riots and terrorism etc.

Environmental Factors

Now, suppose a class of Vedanta is going on and there is constant loud noises, scuffle or murder – takes place – is it possible to carry on the class any further?

Therefore, if we can do anything to decrease even a pinch of terrorism, pollution – we do it by all means. Otherwise, we go ahead with graceful acceptance of the general situation – choosing ways of least conflicts and adjust ourselves. Remember that prayer? We saw earlier about acceptance and asking for wisdom to know the difference between what I can change and what I can't.

(5) The fifth factor from which stress comes is Feeling of lack of Love and Appreciation

I need approval and love is one of the main issues. This is not a personal – -psychological problem – it is universal problem and it is also a spiritual problem.

From my self-consciousness – self-judgement comes giving me notions that – I am insignificant, nobody loves me, nobody wants me, I am small, limited being and so on… Then I blame – my circumstances and from the depth of my heart I cry "WHY ME?" – this is also universal problem. Then I go for self-improvement. I try to change me and the world around and want to be complete. I constantly endeavour for that but any number of the efforts do not put me there. And I always remain a wanting person "I want… I want… I want…" And I go on judging myself a small, inadequate, incomplete.

Vedanta addressed to this basic problem. It states that "self-disapproval" is wrong. As long as one tries to change the world – including – his/her BMS complex – in attempt to be happy and complete – he/she is not going to succeed, because there is no connection between what he/she wants and what he/she does. All the objects of the world are inert. They have no capacity to give you either pain or pleasure.

If I want to be free from the sense of inadequacy, unhappiness and insecurity – I will have to know "myself." Unless I know my true nature – completeness is not gained. And to know my – "Self" I need to have certain particular qualifications. I must have pure mind and to achieve pure mind – there is only one way – and that is performing duties with "Yajna spirit" – keeping with law of Dharma. Dharma is doing right in any given situation. Any amount of -pressure – of desires should not take you for a ride.

Human being is given free will in performing action but he/she has no any right or choice on the result of the action. The law of Karma (action) takes care of the result. You can perform, may not perform or perform the same differently – any given action – using your unique gift – discrimination. But ones the action performed – the result can be of four types (a) Your expected result (b) More than you have expected. (c) Less than you expected. (d) Totally unexpected

The popular stanza of Bhagvad Geeta says

कर्मण्येवाधिकारस्ते मा फलेषु कदाचन ।
मां कर्मफलहेतुर्भूर्मा ते संगोऽस्त्वकर्मणि ।।
[BH. G. 2-47]

You have right in performing action – not in its result. Therefore, you don't do action thinking about its result and (at the same time) may your inclinations – don't be in not – performing actions.

This is largely interpreted as – action is to be performed without expectation. Can any action be performed without expectation? It is impossible. This stanza states that – using your discrimination perform action according to the law of Dharma – that is – do right thing in a given situation – you are free in performing any action but you have no right on its result. Therefore, accept the [result] – fruit of your karma (action) with attitude as you have in prasadam – [consecrated object.] Now this consecrated object may be a pinch of ash, a teaspoon of holy water, a flower, may be a leaf of basil or it may be a big sized sweet piece full of dry fruits – you accept it with respect, without complaint – happily – similarly – when the result of any given action is taken care by Ishwara (God) – and God is in form of law of karma here – you accept it – just like you accept the consecrated objects. You accept the result of any given action – as a consecrated object – as the result of your actions is also coming from an altar. This will free you from the tension of insistence for result of your actions and gives you equanimity, serenity of mind. There are so many variables affecting outcome of action and you have no any control over such variables. You have to accept the result – but if you accept it with attitude as you have in consecrated objects – in accepting the result of your actions – this changed attitude changes the whole picture. It frees you from oppressive pressure and frustration of results of your actions.

Stress comes from within

All the objects of the world are inert. They have no capacity to give you either pain or pleasure, joy or sorrow, gain or loss, victory or defeat. It is the way of viewing the thing and liking and disliking and are just one's mind's projections.

Everyone wants to become uninterruptedly happy. Your basic natural inclination is to be happy always. But – is any object in the world be identified as "happiness"? Happiness is not available as an object. Music makes me happy – at the same time the same music is hated by some another one! One likes certain sweet – his own brother just refuses to take it in his plate. And there are so many factors affecting whether the object or situation is going to give you happiness or creates a problem. Besides you are subjected to your mood also. You may not be comfortable in the experience of same situation with which you had experienced it at that time. All the objects and situations please you according to your likes and dislikes -for the time being. No object, no situation can have content of comfort and happiness. It seems that happiness is centred upon object but actually the happiness is centred upon – "I". If it has been centred upon object than that object must give happiness to every person and to one person all the time – but that is not the case. The same object I liked very much – can become an object of my hatred! Then what can be the real source of happiness? The source of happiness is centred upon "I". You say "I am happy". Can happiness be obtained in any particular part of your body? Do you ever say "my index finger is happy?" "I" – consciousness (Aatma) is the real source of happiness – rather the intrinsic nature of consciousness is happiness. And so – every human being's natural urge is to become happy.

The nature of fire is hot. Fire can't get rid of hotness as long as an it is there – the intrinsic quality of that object will not go away.

If sadness is the nature of the "I" – it can never go away – not even for a fraction of a moment. But it does go away. I am happy daily when I go to sleep. In sleep I become free from all my problems. When I wake-up I say "I slept nicely" Even in deep sorrowful bereavement – in sleep I don't feel pang of pain and feel happy. Everyone likes to go to sleep – nobody complains about sleep – therefore it must be a happy experience for all.

When you enjoy music, beautiful butterflies/birds, smile of a sleeping child, glorious sun rise and sun set, sky full of bright stars – such situation/objects capture your attention and for the time being you forget all your problems. You accept yourself and the world as they are and your mind becomes free from complaint – you feel happy and free. Besides, any knowledge, discovery, good task completed successfully give you happiness.

Thus, we do feel happiness – if my intrinsic nature is sadness – it doesn't go away even for a smallest fraction of a moment. I cannot remain being unhappy. I want to get rid of sadness always and as early as possible – therefore by inquiry – I may discover that perhaps I need not "become" happy – may be "I am" the source of happiness. Happiness is the intrinsic nature of "I". I am always a happy being, complete and limitless existence. Only thing is this, that because of ignorance, because of my identification with my body – mind – sense complex and the roles I play in life – I do not know "I". The knowledge of my true nature (my Self) can free me from all my tension, pressures and stress.

Thus, by understanding – stress can be managed well. A well – managed stress has its own certain advantages.

[A] Advantages of Stress

- **With well managed stress efficiency increases.**
  - Motivation rate becomes high – resulting into better performance and increase in productivity.
  - With well managed stress, one becomes more and more mature. Maturity is development of subtle aspects of discrimination – power.
- **Mobilization of resources takes place**
  - Inter personal relations become better in family – for example – illness, childbirth, bereavement etc. In community– natural calamities like earthquake, flood, cyclones, riots etc. In nation – aggression of other country. Physiological toning up occurs.

If stress is not managed well – it results in – frustration, depression, dejection, sometimes suicidal tendency, anger either towards oneself or family or the system. And if these feelings are not constrained – may result in exhaustion, heart diseases, mental/psychological problems and one may break down physically, mentally, emotionally, socially, morally and spiritually. Therefore, one must cope with the stress.

Four Factors Indicating Coping Ability – The coping ability of any individual depends on Capacity to withstand stress. One will have to know, accept and get used to the stress. As an individual I should take into account the reality of my limitations. Being recognized that only – I will have certain attitude towards those unpleasant situations.

[B] Attitude and Value System

There are two kind of attitudes – positive and negative – Vedanta uses words – right and wrong – and subjective and objective -instead of positive and negative. Always try to have right – attitude i.e., Predominantly objective attitude. I desire and plan (which may be wrong) to fulfil it – taking into account my limitations, limited knowledge, limited power, limited resources, lack of power – in controlling known and unknown and hidden variables, naturally I must be ready to face a situation that is not acceptable. I judge, I value myself in the sense what I am getting for all my efforts – is entirely different from my expectation. The problem of failure is here only – not elsewhere. Outscoring my expectation is very rare happening. I expected to achieve and achieved the same, – much more than expected is very rare phenomenon. Usually, things are always less than expected, even opposite totally sometimes. So be as much as objective. You have economic, psychological, social and spiritual value system of your own and being a self-conscious person, you have complexes and pattern of reaction in a given situation. But always remember to see the things objectively and to act – not react.

The negative [wrong] attitudes like anger, jealousy, greed, dejection etc. just happen. You cannot get angry consciously. If I say, let us all become angry for next two minutes, this is just not possible. But when anger happens – to have emotional adjustment not to come under its spell, to act and not to react is human privilege. By developing emotional maturity human being can do it.

– It is not only unhappiness but extreme of happiness also causes stress. Therefore, the magnitude of the distress and in happy events magnitude of elation both are to be controlled. In Bhagvad Geeta Bhagvan Sree Krishna says [in stanza no. 70 of chapter-2] that the one attains peace into whom all desires enter as waters enter into the ocean, which filled from all sides, remains – unmoved – but not the desirer of desires. One can achieve contentment with understanding and knowing one's self – that, happy events do not cause too much elation and shocking events do not cause severe depression.

[C] Find Out Solution

Problem which has no solution can't be called a problem. There are always alternatives and options to any given problem. Therefore– find out solution of your problem. There may be a way out. These are few points about coping techniques.

[D] Coping Techniques

To cope with stress:

[a]   Keep your goals clear with priorities.

[b]   Develop skill, abilities and strong determination to achieve your goal.

[c]   Check your motivation – whether or not your motivation is totally selfish. Motivation should be constructive. If you give more and more to others – you are more contributor than consumer – the process of giving others contributes in improving self, office, organization, institution, city, state, nation. Society and maintains harmony.

[d]   Internal Recognition. – That is true that I need approval and love from the world around and that's the main issue but through seeking approval of others I seek my own approval. Everybody knows without being taught what is right and what is wrong. Therefore, whenever I do break this universal law of doing right in any given situation – I can conceal it from others but not from myself. As doing wrong is naturally against – my nature I develop split personality causing much stress to

me. If I act according to the universal law of doing right in any given situation – that only can give me internal recognition and strength.

This is one of technique – very effective in reducing and even in preventing stress.

[E] Read Good Books

This is one of the very effective technique – in reducing and also preventing stress. Reading good books is a form of good company.

In the realm of literature of the world -there flowing a full holy river like Ganga (of good literature) and also not worthy to read "like material" also. Therefore, while choosing -one will have to be vigilant. There is reading which can increase your stress but also there are huge good reading available. A -good book is the best friend of one. There is a great difference between the eager person who wants to read a book and a tired, confused person who wants a book to read.

[F] Health

There is one dictum in Gujarati "Pahalu sukh te jate narya" meaning that "The first and the most important happiness is good health". Ill health causes much stress. Therefor try to live a self – disciplined, regular life. Cut·down/stop drinking, smoking. If necessary – take regular medicines for diseases like hypertension, diabetes etc. Go for regular check -up and don't forget physical exercise. Dhyanam [meditation] is extremely useful for maintaining your physical and mental health.

[G] Cultivate Creative Hobbies

Cultivate hobbies like– music, painting, sports, gardening, cooking etc. Such creative hobbies tremendously help in relieving tension – and -stress.

A tired dejected person returns home in the evening and declares to family members that please, don't bother me – leave me alone. I am going to retire – now I am tired very much.

Right at the same time his friend comes and asks him to accompany him to play volleyball. In one moment his all tiredness disappears and he plays one and half hour and returns home fresh and happy.

It is important to create a hobby in your life or the art to convert any work into a hobby.

[H] Laugh

Don't miss laughing. How big, important, great responsible person you may be – grab opportunity of open loud laughter. Recommendation is six time for 30 seconds per day.

[I] Find Out Good Friends

Find out such friends to whom you can talk everything without hiding anything. This friend can be your mother, father, brother, sister. Spouse, neighbour or friend. If you can-not find out your true friend in any one of them, make prayer – a regular routine of your life. Remember, HE\SHE [ISHWARA] is always there for you – eager to relate to you. Ishwara can be the best friend of yours.

[J] Always Count Yours Blessings and Not Curses and

[K] Reduce Desires – Desires – bind you.

My life of – "becoming" – is because of desires. My mind constantly sings "I want" "I want" "I want" – My unfulfilled desires become fulfilled desires – but all desires cannot be fulfilled and my core person goes on wanting and wanting more. My mind never becomes empty of heap of unfulfilled desires and it is logically impossible for a person to be happy and at the same time to be wanting. These heap of unfulfilled desires in my mind results in frustration, unhappiness, dissatisfaction and obsession. Unless I clear my mind from this garbage it will not allow me to live peaceful – tension free life. Though to desire is a human privilege – I will have to use my discrimination in desiring. I will have to avoid binding desires. I will have to remove garbage from my mind. Then only I can live a happy peaceful, tension free life.

Again – whenever I get my desired object – it gives rise to excitement – then the object creates fear of losing it and if it is lost – that causes sorrow. Now think, excitement, fear and sorrow – either of these – can give you peace and equipoise of mind? Vedanta tells it "YOGA-KSHEMA".

(योग – क्षेम) If I act and accept the results of my actions with attitude of accepting consecrated object (प्रसादम्) I leave my "YOGA-KSHEMA" to the laws of nature to take care and Lord Shree Krishna has promised that for such person he will bear all responsibility of looking after his\her\it's **YOGA-KSHEMA.**

Therefore Cultivate

Right——————— Views – and – Values.

Right——————— Intentions.

Right——————— Speech.

Right——————— Action.

Right——————— Living.

Right——————— Efforts.

Right——————— Thinking.

And always try to contribute in maintaining harmony of the universe.

OM

*****

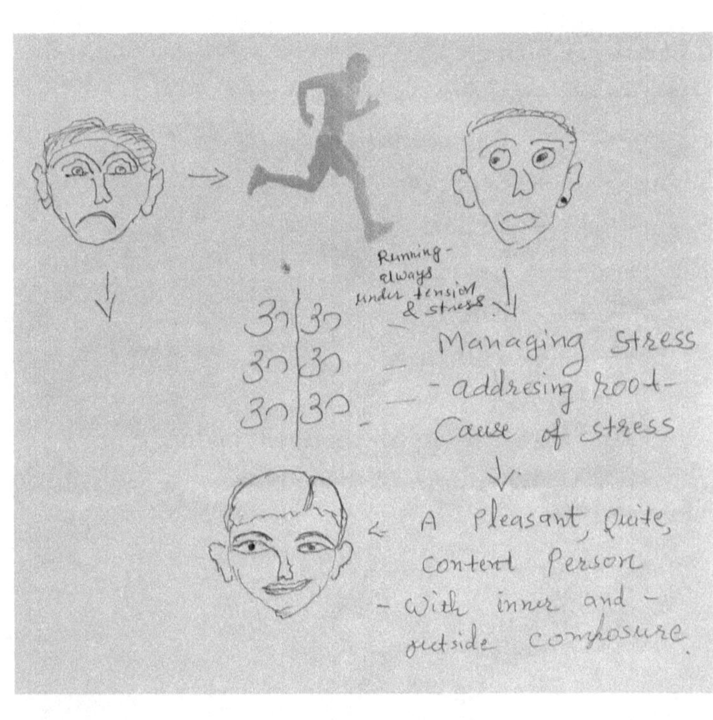

Running -
always
under tension
& stress.
३० / ३०
३० / ३०
३० / ३०
Managing Stress
- addresing root-
Cause of stress
A Pleasant, Quite,
content Person
- with inner and -
outside composure.

Relating to the World is Relating to the Ishwara

"We do not have many Gods. We do not even have one God. We have ONLY GOD."

– Swami Dayanandji Maharaj.

You will have to relate. You can-not live without relating to your surroundings. And surprisingly almost all our problems are also related to the "relating" to the world. Because this relating only gives rise to the feeling of hurt and guilt which are the sole cause of our sorrows in life.

During our three months course on Upanishad KATHOPANISHAD – at Rishikesh -Dayanand Pitam on bank of river Gangaji-a sadhu came, prostrated before Pujya Swamiji. Swamiji asked him to sit before him and they talked in south Bhartiya language. Then he told that he wants to perform some tapas – this time he spoke in Hindi language – and he wants to live in some nice quite place preferably on bank of Gangaji. Swamiji remained silent for some time -then told him that on way beyond Uttarkashi, going left a bit away and near Ganga there is one kutia and presently it is available as nobody is living there. Then he was asked to meet an Ashram head in Uttarkashi and inform him that Swamiji has sent him for this purpose. Next day that sadhu departed for his venture. After a week that sadhu appeared in Ashram again.

"Didn't you tell you want to perform tapas for a month? Swamiji asked him What happened? Why you returned? Was the place not suitable?"

"SWAMIJI, That is not the case – the place was very quiet and beautiful as I wished to have for my purpose but there was much disturbance." "Didn't you just told me that the place was very quiet?'

"Yes Swamiji, it was. But right from early morning – so many birds made noises and there were so many different kinds of birds they didn't allow me to perform my Sadhana"

Swamiji just smiled – for his not completing his tapas for such a reason. And that sadhu returned to south Bharat where he was living. Thus, if one goes away amongst forest or mountain -or -anywhere he\she will have to relate to his\her surroundings. Therefore, wherever you are – you will have to relate with your surrounding world. And you will have to relate with changed attitude. No any action is involved here but only knowledge is involved. To avoid the feeling of hurt and guilt – remember that – whomever you are relating – you are always relating to Ishwara -e. g. Ishwara in form of laws of nature. Relating to Ishwara is nothing but -devotion and devotion is nothing but love with respect.

'But how this is possible? When most of the world is too much for me. So thankless. So unappreciative? Here some analysis is required.

Some people have art of relating and they are the most successful in the world. These people know that it is very important and rewarding part of their lives and nothing wrong in that. They have all worldly nicest things with them – wealth, name, fame and relations. But if you ask them – "Are you free from sorrow and sense of incompleteness and insecurity?" The honest answer is bound to be "No".

And human life ends with persistent feeling of incompleteness and insecurity amongst comforts.

To be born a human is a rare privilege because of the unique gift of discrimination and the faculty of choice. Human being is endowed with free will – with power to use faculties as wished.

The one who is born as human being with the unique gift of free will and power of discrimination – who is a thinking– mature person will definitely think at some stage of life that there must be some solution of my persistent problem of sense of insecurity, incompleteness, inadequacy and sorrows. If in spite of all efforts to come out of this sense, in spite of obtaining and accomplishing everything– all pleasures, securities and comforts -if I cannot be free from the sense of sadness and sorrows and the intense wish for constant happiness, security and happiness and completeness which are naturally there with me without putting any effort to develop it – then -perhaps may be -my basic nature be secure and happy? May be my intrinsic nature is already secure and happy? "I" the self is happiness? If a human being dies without having this kind of inquiry in life – the rest of the things in lives of animals and humans are same. Except human being no one has this faculty of thinking and choice. Choice is everything. Whenever there is possibility of choice – there only can be two kinds of choices – one is right choice, another is wrong choice. Human being's interaction with world is not totally programmed like animal kingdom. It comes by choice and there should be common basis Dharma which is acceptable to all.

This Dharma is not religion, having a personal GOD. It is not religious customs and traditions – but it is that Dharma, which exists in the creation. It is not different from Ishwara I. e. laws of nature. As the time and space exist, as the law of gravity exists – the Dharma exists. As you sense the law of gravity – you sense Dharma. As we saw earlier Dharma is defined "Doing right [or doing what is to be done whether you like it or not] in a given situation." And as the Dharma exists in the creation every human being knows without being taught what is write and what is wrong. What I expect from others I.e. love, care, honour, compassion, telling only truth, no stealing etc. – others expect the same from me and that is the secret of knowing Dharma without being taught. If it's like that – everyone knows about right and wrong – why human being transgresses the limit of Dharma and invites papam? That is because of pressure of desires. You misuse your faculties and do wrong kind of choice transgressing the Dharma. As you have to obey the law of gravity, – You must obey the law of Dharma. Fall from a height – not believing in the law of gravity, you break your bones, similarly you break the law of Dharma -rub against it and you will have to suffer.

A monkey baby and birds also – sense the law of gravity, therefore baby monkey holds on tight to its mother when she jumps from one tree to another. Birds use their wings hard until they rich high in sky and the force of gravity – decreases. They sense natural laws but rest of the in their lives – what is to be done – is programmed. They don't have the faculty of choice. But human being has faculty of choice and freedom of using the faculty as wished. And so – human can use this faculty in right way or in a wrong way. Thus human being can transgress the borders of law of Dharma – and being a natural law I. e. Ishwara nobody can disobey these Laws. one disobeys and pays in terms of sorrows. The law of Dharma is totally unavoidable therefore – if I don't want to be sad, unhappy, insecure -and want to be free from sense of hurt and guilt in my interaction with the world I will have to follow the law of nature i.e. Dharma. I will have to do right only – whether I like it or not in any given situation. I will have to do only appropriate things while relating to the objects \individuals\ situations. I will have to care not only for human beings but also for all my surroundings including elements like air, water, space, earth and animals, birds, trees, plants etc.

The ecology does not end only in preventing extinction of birds and animals and pollution by petroleum products, holes in ozone layer, noise pollution, over population problems, receding forests etc. Vedanta go ahead and say – pollution also takes place by your even smallest improper, inappropriate thought, deed and speech because by doing so you break the harmony of the universe.

President Abdul Kalam writes in introduction of his book "Wings of Fire" that "Each individual creature on this beautiful planet is created by God to fulfil a particular role". This is the very thing Vedanta says.

Ponder on Yourself

I must think why I am here, in this place, in this situation? And in a human body? Not a tree, bird or animal – why? The Universe is but one i.e. whatever is here is – woven in one single thread i.e. Consciousness – only names and forms are different, as the gold is but one -the forms and names of different ornaments are many.

Whatever I think, speak and do are bound to affect the whole Universe. If I disturb the harmony of the Universe by disobeying the law of nature i.e. Ishawara. I cannot remain without disturbing my own harmony, my own happiness, my own security. Whatever I am, whoever I am, whatever role I am playing [may be small and insignificant.] I am unique and unavoidable. I – am – always assigned to carry great responsibilities on my shoulders – of maintaining the harmony, happiness and purity of the universe. I will have to understand that, if I am sad and – incomplete, there is something wrong in my thinking process, my understanding, my attitude. I may be wrong in my conclusion about myself that I am unhappy, insecure, limited – and incomplete. I will have to see that there is no connection between what I do and what I want basically. When I – can't "BE" – complete by living a life of becoming and basically I want to be complete always, constantly and naturally – I must be complete NOW and if it is so -why I am not experiencing the completeness? On the contrary I always feel myself incomplete and insecure. The scriptures say – that it is because of your ignorance about your true nature – your real self – i.e. "Atma" – that is because of your search for completeness where it is not – means – outside yourself. Know yourself – you are the most complete, secure, happy being. And to know thyself you must have certain qualifications. You will have to live a life of Dharma which is there in the creation as a law of nature and you know it without being taught. Follow the life of Dharma, or break it and suffer. There is no alternative choice.

Therefore, you must remember always that whenever you relate with any object – individual or situation you are relating to the Ishwara only. And relating to Ishwara is nothing but prayer and devotion.

How to Assimillate This Fact?

The scriptures say about creation of the universe that "सर्व अभवत्" "Sarvam abhavat'. "He/she [Ishwara] became all". Here– it is not said – (असृजत्) "asrujat" [He/she/ it – Ishwara created] – This clearly conveys that creator is not different from the creation. The maker and made are but one and the same. This is fact – but is not easy to assimilate. Therefore, scriptures give two examples to make us understand.

Things put together – intelligently – to serve a purpose is a creation. The world seems to be a very intelligent creation. No any discipline – any knowledge is left which has not been used in this creation – means discipline and knowledge known to us – then even – still there are many things unknown to the mankind.

Any creation presupposes knowledge. And there must be material for the creation and there must be a creator. This creator must be conscious being. Inert can-not create. For example, take creation of the clay pot. There must be a creator – a pot – maker, who must have skill and knowledge of how to make a clay pot, and there must be clay – the material. The pot maker by using the knowledge and skill, creates a clay pot from the material – clay. Now the world must have been created by a creator – say Ishwara – the supreme conscious being who must be omniscient – all knowing.

But How is It Created?

From which material? And before creation – when even space and time also yet not created – where the material can exist? Hear scriptures say सर्वं अभवत् ("Sarvam Abhavat".) HE\SHE/IT [The Ishwara] became the universe. In creation of the world-here – the intelligent cause [the creator] and the material cause [the creation] are not different but one and the same. The creator Ishawara by him\her/it -self – became this world. Whatever is here – is nothing but one without the second. Therefore, there is not ONE GOD – nor many GODS – but ONLY GOD – and -and nothing except GOD. Whatever "IS" is Ishwara only.

How this can assimilated? Now please, think about your dream experience. Dream experience comes from sleep. In sleep there is no subject – object differentiation. No time, no space. Before your subject – object encounter in dream – you will have to go to sleep. This condition is comparable to the condition prevailing before creation of the world. In sleep you don't have subject -object – time – space concept. Then YOU create dream reality. In your dream – there may be your friend, yourself, river, ocean, forests, mountains, sun, stars, moon – anything – can be created – but only your known objects only. Think – from where all these dream objects -which you consider real during your dream – come? From which material? These objects come from – yourself only. YOU are the CREATOR – and at the time of experiencing dream you don't think – them to be unreal. They look as real [at that time] as your encounter with this world in your waking state. But then all the objects you create in your dream – go back – to yourself. In the same way – the world is also created, sustained and resolved – by Ishwara. As your waking – sleeping – dreaming cycles go on, similarly for the world creation – resolution – creation – resolution – such cycles – go on.

Another example is spider. As spider produces and takes back threads, the world is also produced and resolved by natural laws – Ishwara.

Besides, everything is given to us. Body, mind, intellect, memory, parentage, birthplace, friends, relatives, circumstances, job stars, profession, moon, sun, sky, air, water, time, space, earth everything is given to us. Nothing new can be created by us. We can just discover what was not known till now but was existing here.

Now here you are and there – before you – an object, individual or situation – to which you are to relate. And there is space between you and your object of relating.

Your body – mind -sense complex is given to you, the object – individual – situation is given to you. The space differentiating you and the object – individual – situation -given to you. Therefore, whatever you encounter with is nothing but creation including yourself and the creator and the creation are one and the same. The intelligent cause and the material cause are not different – whether like it or not there is no choice. You have to relate and whenever you relate you relate with the Ishwara only. Yourself, the object you are relating with or individual or circumstances are not separate from Ishwara. Therefore, you and the object of your relating are not different from each other and therefore whenever you relate – you relate with Ishwara only.

Therefore, whatever you do, think and say is nothing but relating to Ishawara i. e. laws of nature. And laws of nature – Ishwara – can-not be disobeyed. Disobey – you will have to suffer.

You work anywhere – in hospital, office, company or home – is nothing but relating to the Ishwara and therefore devotion, you play role of a father, mother, son, daughter, sibling, spouse, citizen, employer, employee – is devotion, you play, sing, cook is devotion. Even you steal, cheat, lie is also devotion [but here the law– Dharma is violated]. There is no time, no place – when and where you are separated from your maker you are constantly relating to Ishwara only.

If – you know and assimilate this fact – can there be any discordant note – when you are constantly singing beautiful devotional song – of relating to the world i.e. Ishawara? And when that's so – where is the problem of guilt and hurt? When there is no guilt and hurt – there is no problem of sorrow.

Many other solutions have been suggested related to the problems arising in relating to the world – they prove to be patch work. ONLY right understanding and knowledge of self – give – solution to this universal problem of sense of insecurity. Incompleteness and limitation because of feeling of "lacking something". When it is clearly understood that relating to the world – relating to your surrounding – is nothing but relating to the Ishwara – you always relate to anything – anybody you will relate with right way and with confidence. You know, now, that relating with the world is nothing but devotion.

OM

*****

In the world -
there are - two things
I and everything-
else. I is Atma -
(Consciousness) and
everything else is inert -
but not separate from - Atma - (Consciousness)
Omni Present
Vishnu

तत्त्वमसि ।
"You Are That"
"That" is Omni-
Potent - Omni Present.
Vishnu

Universe is -
Pervaded by the
Brahman
- So with -
whatever You
relate - You relate
with Vishnu -
(Ishwara)

Chapter 3

Hurt and Guilt Management

"We can-not direct the wind but can adjust our Sail."
— Swami Chinmayanandji Saraswati

In life its experience for many – coming in contact with – others – who -are behaving in hurting manner. One can hurt you by words, by tone of the words spoken or even by silence – total or partial silence. This may result in sorrows. And there are only two main reasons for sorrow – hurt and guilt.

"How can he/she behave in this manner?"How can use such language?"and you get hurt. Second cause for sorrow is omission. "Why I didn't do this or that? It was worth doing. – It was my duty. How I missed it?"– Omission. And "Why I did that? How could I? What happened with me that I lost my discrimination power? Was that me who used such words?"– Commission. And these both giving rise to the sense of being guilty.

Think, is there any other reason for sorrow? "Yes" you can say – "Death of your near and dear." But death is an unavoidable truth of life. The universal conclusion of the core person is "I am mortal" – mortal means total – dissemination. Mortal is subjected to time. "I am born." And the rule is "born is gone" Every born one grows old and dies. One doesn't like to become old and can-not accept aging process and death. Vedanta disapproves the idea of death and dissemination. We will see about this in the next chapter. But the fact is – one wants to live a day more happily without being ignorant.

This sense of sorrow, "lacking something" feeling, notion of being mortal and feeling hurt and guilt – is cantered on I. Does your body interpret about these? No never. You will have to conclude "I feel I am drowned in sorrow." Sorrow is cantered upon I. Vedanta explains that – human being creates an opinion about oneself because of the complete self – consciousness. What are they? "I am unhappy, limited, incomplete and mortal. I am in sorrow. I am insignificant." Etc. And there seems to be an element of truth. One feels incomplete- – in sense of money, power, appearance, relationships, fame etc – and one disapproves oneself. Because of such conclusions one's self-image gets damaged and gives rise to dissatisfaction. The one blames circumstances or some near and dear for the same and his/her self-esteem gets hurt.

Then one can't stand ignorance. If you remain ignorant for ever – there is no problem. But you grow physically, psychologically and mentally and get exposed to the world. As you know more and more – and as much more you know -the more you come to know that – what you don't know. And you can't accept this so again your self-esteem gets hurt and you suffer with non – healing wounds giving rise to complexes.

I become victim of hurts and guilts because I consider myself doer and enjoyer of action. Therefore, if I am not doer and enjoyer of action then hurt and guilt can-not touch me. Therefore, hurt and guilt affect me in proportion of my "I ness" – ego. The scars of the hurt feelings is in proportion of my "I ness" -ego -which is degree of identification with my emotional world. Wounds created by hurt and guilt are as deep as our notion of being superior.

Bhagvad Geeta mainly conveys message – "मां शुचः।" "maa shuchh" meaning "Don't be in sorrow – be free from sorrow." Actually, Bhagvad Geeta dismisses – your notion about – being a doer and enjoyer. Then who is doing actions? – am I not doing? If I am not the doer and enjoyer – then who is? You may ask. And Bhagvad Geeta explains "You are doer -seemingly but you are as though doer." You are enjoyer – but you are "as though" enjoyer." HOW? You can ask – and answer is – the doer ship and enjoyer -ship are because of your identification with your BMS complex. You will have to understand that there is no difference between the three – the doer or knower and the object of your knowledge or doing and the knowledge. Understand clearly that you are a doer and enjoyer – is nothing but just a notion. For that you will have to know the true nature of yourself. The reason of this notion is ignorance about your intrinsic nature of yourself. When this notion of your being doer and enjoyer will go away by knowledge of your "Aananda swaroop" and being non doer/non enjoyer nature– then only you can become permanently free from feeling of hurt and guilt. Sadness is there because of wrong thinking process. Sorrow is not in situations and happenings but it is in your understanding. You consider yourself victim of unhappiness and incompleteness and cry from the depth of your heart "Why me?" This is not a personal problem – it is a universal problem.

With this analysis also – till one assimilate this knowledge – hurt and guilt remain part of life and cause sorrows and pain. One's whole life can become a series of efforts of saving oneself from hurt and guilt. As everyone wants to be happy – none wants sorrow – there must be a permanent resolution to this problem – and that is knowing true nature of oneself. For that one has to learn scriptures – spending a length of time at the feet of – srotriya teacher – and learn Bhagvad Geeta and Upanishads [Vedanta]. The WORDS of VEDANTA are the only means to reveal your true – intrinsic nature to you. These word – mirror only introduce you to your true "YOU." And you need to be qualified enough to understand and assimilate what's being taught. To have this qualification is also rare. Therefore, one will have to learn to manage the feelings of hurts and guilts.

As we saw earlier if you confront with hurting person – by luck or by choice and you have capacity – to accept such person – then this is a grace.

Now – look at this—Love is surrender. Love is always unconditional – unlike attachment. Love never demands control. Love gives full freedom and accepts others as they are, one may immensely enjoy your company but also solitude in your absence. The right attitude is "I am happy and make others happy. I am free and so you are too". This attitude helps one to grow and the same thing can destroy too. It is like sharpening wheel. If the knife is put on the rotating band at right angle – then it will get well sharpened, – if not then it may become flat blunt instead.

Vedanta teaches to fall in love with yourself. If I can love myself with my limitations – I can love others with their limitations.

When you confront with hurting person in life and you have accepted the person because of either love or by compassion – and you have capacity to tolerate – and you must have – strength and understanding – also lots of courage and patience also needed. In response to your care, concern and reaching out actions to help him/her – there will be no sign of reciprocation and improvement. Then you will have to understand and take it in this way that the individual can-not behave differently than what he/she does. You will have to see that – behind such behaviour – he/she has some pain, some unhealed wounds inside. There are unresolved complexes in unconscious – may be some childhood trauma, some wounds, some scars. Now, here a quiet, content and understanding mind is very useful against such hurting behaviour. One has to develop strength to accept and has to get used to stand such behaviour. It is very much possible that, your sympathy, your friendly compassionate attitude to reach out may be taken for granted. Particularly this happens when the person is convinced that you are not going away – you are not going to leave them behind and you are going to be always available. When this situation takes place – you have to be much – strong – to stand and tolerate such behaviour. Now – you may have decided to help and heal the person or you may have accepted the situation as your luck – and you -may have gone to an extent to help such immature – attitude because you must have accepted the one with his/her limitations. But it may happen that – the person may prove to be totally insensitive and has failed to understand your efforts to help him/her and just go on behaving in the same manner and this may be giving you pain. Then even if you can accept and continue – this is your extraordinary strength – inside and outside and also a kind of grace or may -be you have surrendered to the situation considering this – to be your stars. BUT if it is beyond your tolerance power – you have stretched your strength up to your maximum -and it becomes beyond your tolerance – you will have to manage your hurts. You will have to take steps and you have right to save yourself-therefore first you keep the relationship formal and save you from pain. You will have to conclude that he/she is just like that or intentionally behaving this way? Anyway – you can always save yourself from such an immature person.

First of all -try to talk about this with that person. Tell him/her clearly "This hurts me". Then even if he/she continues behaving in the same manner– you have to draw strict boundaries. To manage your hurt you have to take stern steps instead of only thinking about the same – this also will need courage and understanding.

Study of scriptures – Bhagvad – Geeta-can help a lot. Bhagvad Geeta is not – conveying religious mandates. Bhagvad Geeta addresses basic problems of human life which are universal and shows how to live a successful, Secure and complete human life – and these are the basic want of everyone. Whatever one does is always to fulfil these desire – the desire to feel complete – but the endeavours are being done in wrong way. Bhagvad Geeta points out actions performed with right attitude – that is – Karmayoga – which prepares you to face any situation in right way – at the same time maintaining the inner content and composure. Geeta teaches to prepare your mind which is ready – and strong – with discipline, sadhana, and prayerful attitude – giving you inner strength and purification – also fearlessness. All this puts you on the royal path of fulfilling success through – activities performed with right attitude. Karmayoga is -in short [We will see in details later in the same series about it] sameness of mind in accepting results of any action and doing right in any given situation. Vedanta uses words-"right" and "wrong" – not good and bad which are subjective.

- If one listens to Katha [Events of Avatara – incarnation of Ishawara – and his/her stuties] -that also can help.
- You will have to relieve yourself from pleasing others.
- Remember, large heartedness is good but also know "enough is enough."
- Thinking of others and putting them first is a sign of growth – but nurturing "child mind" – and nurturing selfish attitude of an adult will not help either that person nor you – there is loss on both sides.
In life we are doing three types of journey.
- Journey in space, Journey in time, Journey in becoming.
- In all these journey we must know – "when to drop?" and particularly in the journey of becoming and accomplishing.
- Lastly – it will be important to know that Bhartiya Vedic society was the heathiest and wealthiest society. That society was devoid – of any thief or any bagger and was devoid of competition – -living happily with the least struggle -was based on performing duties. The cultural value was duty.

An individual – performing his/her duties of the role he or she – playing-was fulfilling rights of another and the other individual performing his/her duties fulfilling rights of the one mentioned first. And all performing their duties properly with right attitude – fulfilled rights of all.

Human life is described by the scripture having – four – phases – considering life span -100 years. Each phase is of 25 years. The first phase is called (ब्रह्मचर्याश्रम) "Brahmcharyashram". It is a student life, the second one is (गृहस्थाश्रम) "Gruhsthasham" – house holder phase. The 3rd phase -from 50 to 75 years is वानप्रस्थाश्रम) – "Vanprasthashram" – now one starts withdrawing slowly from activities and starts to live introspective life. If during this phase an individual lives with readiness to grow and analyse his and others' experiences with discriminative attitude he/she may attain maturity enough to withdraw from attachments and bondages, understands the reality of worldly objects and situations and proceeds towards enlightenment. He/she can see their mind's notions and complexes and may neutralize them and become emotionally stabilized and mature. He/she becomes ready for freedom from worldly afflictions and excess of "I NESS". This maturity is nothing but renunciation. If one attains this kind of maturity and knowledge of true nature of self which is (सच्चिदानंद) "Sachhidananda" [Sat, chit, aananda swarupa-] Sat means TRUTH– Chit is memory and Ananda is happiness – or he/she doesn't reach up to that stage – then even the one will be saved from cycles of births and deaths and from the affliction attached with this unending voyage from one body to the another and neutralising their "KARMAPHALAM" [Results of a bunch of their previous karma – to exhaust them they are given that kind of suitable body of animal – bird -insect – any].

Each – phase – of life span has its duties and a way to live a life. Scriptures recommend duties and one lives a dutiful life – performing – his/her duties – easy or hard. Convenient or inconvenient, requiring any sacrifice – small or big – but it is performed with right attitude because it is duty – that individual – grows slowly and attains emotional and spiritual maturity with freedom from bondages while living – becomes free from sense of ownership over objects and proceed towards supreme goal of human life. They become free from conflicts and can maintain inner composure in any circumstances. The one feels complete while living and they don't have to face problem of hurts and guilt. They attain the ultimate goal of successful human life.

This is like a modern factory where – on one end – raw material is put and it made pass through various procedures – when the material comes out – at the other last end in fully "Ready to sell" form. Similarly, if any individual lives all four Ashrams [four phases] according to recommendation of scriptures they become ready for what is called MOKSH.

OM

*****

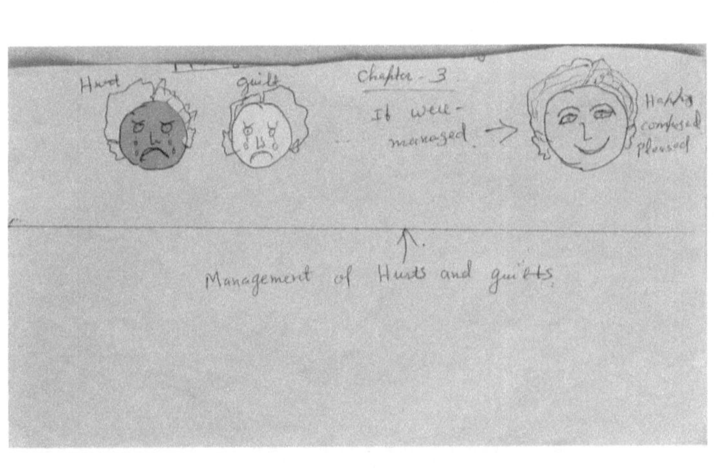

Hurt
guilt
Chapter - 3
If well-managed →
Happy
composed
pleased
Management of Hurts and guilts

Chapter 4

Karmayoga

Do you Want to live a fulfilling, happy and successful life? Then, you will have to redefine definition of Success and have to discover and build your self-esteem.

Success is always equivalent to one's self-esteem Bgagvad Geeta clearly points out activities with right attitude – Karmayoga – which exhaust your mental weakness and dirt and leads to inner strength and composure.

No one – can remain without doing karma for a moment. But here the word "yoga" is important. This word – "YOGA" is derived from dhatu [Sanskrit root] युज् (Yuj.) The word carries meaning here – in this word – Karmayoga – is – "To unite". Therefore, the meaning of the word "Yoga" is "To unite with Karma". But as such every karma is performed by uniting with that karma only. But Karmayoga is to unite with karma with proper attitude.

Human being is given freedom of karma. You may perform any particular action, you can decide – not to perform the same or you can perform it differently. At the same time human being is also given knowledge of what is right and what is wrong without being taught. No education is necessary – all – man or woman, small or big, educated or uneducated know what is right and what is wrong in given situation. If it is so then why people do that is not right? That is because of pressure of राग and द्वेष [likes and dislikes and also मोह: -delusion] The pressure of binding desires is so big that this makes one transgress the boundaries of the Law of Dharma which is given with the creation – as the law of gravitation is given. These laws operate infallibly and impartially – Dharma is defined as "Doing right in any given situation". Please, take to notice that the word used here is right and not good. Good and bad can be subjective but right and wrong remain objective. Here it's also important to see that – no value is absolute.

Bhagvad Geeta is divine song of the Lord – incarnate of Ishwara – SRI KRISHNA – who conveyed this beautiful message to human race through Arjun. Swami Vivekanada said "Geeta is a bouquet composed of beautiful flowers of spiritual truth collected from Upanishads".

Bhagvad Geeta is relevant always for two reasons. Firstly, it talks about the TRUTH and truth can never be negated. Secondly Geeta addresses basic human universal problems.

Arjun was preparing since long for a war of Mahabharat. It was a war like world war – Arjun was to fight with his own people – who walked on path of अधर्म [ADHARMA AND INJUSTICE]. To fight with and punish – such people and particularly rulers is considered duty of a Kshatriya. Arjun was brave, full of valour, the best in archery, mature and sensitive prince. Sri Krishna was very good friend of him. Sri Krishna -himself praises him so many times in Bhagvad Geeta. No one can even think that Arjun had any kind of fear. But when he saw his highly honourable – elders including Bhishma and Guru Dronacharya, own cousin brothers, sons, friends, uncles and so many young soldiers – his heart became full of compassion and he thought – "Is these massive bloodshed is just for a throne? I don't want such throne on which I have to climb corpses of my own people." Out of compassion and thinking about approaching massive blood shed he went into a condition of shock. His bow – named गांडीव "Gandiva" fell down and he sat on sit of his chariot – trembling and perspiring. He declared that he doesn't want to fight. Therefore, in the beginning Sri Krishna said some encouraging, also some sarcastic words but those words went without any effect.

Then Arjun declared himself as student of Sri Krishna – upon whom he had sraddha for his capability of resolving any difficult situation and surrendered to Sri Krishna – saying

शिष्यस्तेऽहं शाधि मां त्वां प्रपन्नम् ।

"I surrender to you -I am your student.
Please, guide me."

Arjun was thinking that all these people would die and he would be responsible for the same and so – if he gets power to rule all the three lokas then even he doesn't want to fight instead he would prefer to live on alms. But he will not prefer to be a cause of such massive destruction.

Sri Krishna said that to fight this war was his duty and without thinking about result – he should fight because to perform duty was his Dharma.

Bhagvan Sri KRISHNA said,

कर्मण्येवाधिकारस्ते मा फलेषु कदाचन ।
मां कर्मफलहेतुर्भूर्मा ते संगोऽस्त्वकर्मणि ।।

**Karmaṇy-evādhikāras te mā phaleṣu kadācana;
mā karma-phala-hetur bhūr mā te saṅgo'stvakarmaṇi.
[BH. G. 2-47]**

Your choice is in action only – never in the result thereof. Do not be the author of action. Let -your attachment not be to inaction.

As we saw -human being is endowed by free will in reference of performing karma. Also -only human being can use faculties as wished. So that there is total freedom and right over choice of action. But once an action – is performed, the result is taken care by the Law of Karma – You don't have choice over the result of action. Ishwara is in form of law. Since human being has freedom of choice of action – this freedom can be used or disused. The doer of the action is responsible for that action as the choice, planning, efforts, revising planning, perseverance—over all these -human has choice. But result depends upon the law of karma. Ishwara is "Karmaphalpradata" – giver of result of actions.

We need to recognise our limitations. Limitation here is not helplessness. Helplessness is felt only if we don't accept our limitations – therefore, it has a negative connotation. But when limitation is acknowledged that is objectively.

Every action is desire based and for fulfilling राग and द्वेष [likes and dislikes]. When it is so, you have figured out which karma will produce which result. But you find that which you had figured out is not that predictable. You also find out that you are getting exactly opposite of what you thought you would get. We have seen earlier that the result falls always into one of the following categories – more than we want, less than we want, opposite of what we want or exactly what we want.

Therefore, Sri Krishna also mention a piece of caution that for that reason there not be your attachment in inaction. When karmas are not to be performed with attachment towards result then how actions are to be performed?

The Karmayoga that Krishna is praising is defined in two ways. The first is – evenness of mind is called Karmayoga-the second is discretion in action is called Karmayoga. Both definitions are to be understood – only then Karmayoga is understood properly.

Lord Krishna praised karmas with special attitude – at the same time praised आत्मज्ञान. [The knowledge of SELF] And Krishna asked Arjun to fight this war for it was his dharma [duty]. It seemed to Arjun that Krishna was saying "knowledge liberates therefore do karma." He thought it was said that "Knowledge is okay and karmayoga is okay". These were seemingly contradictory words. Then Arjun asked Krishna to point out about one thing out of the two which is the best for him to follow. "Because" he said "from your words I understand that – knowledge liberates and karma binds. Why then you want me bound to this karma?

Sree Krishna answered him in the following verse.

लोकेऽस्मिन् द्विविधा निष्ठा पुरा प्रोक्ता मयानघ ।
ज्ञानयोगेन साङ्ख्यानां कर्मयोगेन योगिनाम् ।।

Loke'smin dvi-vidhā niṣṭhā purā proktā mayānagha;
jñāna-yogena sāṅkhyānāṁ karma-yogena yoginām.
[BH. G. 3-3]

O sinless, there are two kind of committed life styles. One is pursuit of knowledge for the renunciates and another is pursuit of action for those who pursue activity. निष्ठा (Nishtha means a committed life style. The word साङ्ख्य saankhya means knowledge and is also used in Bnagvad Geeta by Sri Krishna to mean संन्यास (sanyasa) the life of renunciation. Those who are committed to knowledge are called saankhyas or sanyasis. Saankhya also means BRAHMAN. The life style of renunciation includes – persuasion – of knowledge alone.

Karmayogi performs karmas – does duties with proper attitude and knows clearly that goal is "Shreyas" – moksha. There is no any other aim. If one lives an honest ethical life – a life of Dharma and may be better than Karmayogi – then even karmayogi is different. KARMAYOGA is पुरुषार्थनिश्चय ("Purusharthanishchaya") determination for Moksha [Moksha is liberation from cycles of births and deaths]. Without inclusion of Ishwara and pursuit for jnanam by purity of mind – just – living a life of karmayogi – freedom from cycles of births and deaths and all associated afflictions – can't – be achieved.

It is true that karma binds but karmas performed to neutralise raaga and dweshas [strong likes and dislikes], karmas performed with right attitude for purity of mind and to gain grace of Ishawara and duties performed – whether it is easy or difficult, convenient or inconvenient with prayerful attitude – that become KARMAYOGA.

If a person lives a life of karmayoga then only – sanyasa is possible because without winning over raaga and dwesha – to live a life of sanyasi is not easy nor it becomes successful. Karmayoga is the cause for Jnanyoga – commitment towards knowledge.

Sanyasa is to be understood properly. It is a condition of pure, subtle, limitless – happiness as a result of knowledge of true nature of SELF. This happiness is independent, and it can't – be compared with happy experiences depending on senses and outside objects. This happiness – exists without any cause "निर्निमित्त [causeless]. And it never goes away. There is one विषय सुख ("VISHAY SUKHA") – happiness coming, from sensual experiences. Then there is happiness – as a result of some extraordinary accomplishment like successful invention, honour of some awards or the best performance etc. Then जप japa, ध्यानम्. (Dhyanam) Yoga also give you happiness. But the happiness of knowing the true nature of self is beyond any other kind of happiness. It is called तुरिय सुखम् ("TURIYA SUKHA") and it is different from विषय – सुखम् [sensual] sukha [happiness], विद्या सुखम् and योगसुखम् (Yogasukham). Therefore, sanyasa is not only abandoning everything and wearing saffron attire. Sanyasa is maturity. Sanyasa is looking at objects, situations and individuals objectively. Abandoning attachment is a part of sanyasa but this doesn't mean abandoning loving and meaningful relationships or never using luxurious things – it only means ending dependency on any individual and objects and abandoning ownership. This "Triya sukham – [happiness]" is the best, limitless, non – dependant, beyond senses, unbroken – continuous happiness. It is beyond any other kind of known happiness. Once obtained this happiness doesn't go away. Besides nothing remains to do or to know. Any kind of shocking or unfortunate – situation happens– that can't affect this happiness. This happiness – continuously shines because it is happiness of knowledge of true – intrinsic nature of Self which is SAT CHIT ANANDA. As in any circumstances fire remains hot – hotness being its intrinsic nature. Similarly in any circumstances who has really known the intrinsic nature of SELF – being ANANDA – is not affected by any outside situation. Karmayoga is not direct cause for Moksha [liberation] but without passing through karmayoga it is not possible to be qualified for knowledge. This knowledge require qualification in the form of साधनचतुष्टय "Sadhanchatushtaya" and pure mind – mind free from likes and dislikes -which is prepared by karmayoga.

Sri Krishna gives two clear definitions of karmayoga...

योगस्थःकुरु कर्माणि सङ्गं त्यक्त्वा धनञ्जय ।
सिद्ध्यसिद्ध्योःसमो भूत्वा समत्वं योग उच्यते ।।

Yoga-sthaḥ kuru karmāṇi saṅgaṁ tyaktvā dhanañjaya;
siddhy-asiddhyoḥ samo bhūtvā samatvaṁ yoga ucyate.
[BH. G. 2-48]

O Dhananjaya, perform action remaining steadfast in yoga, remaining same in success and failure alike and abandoning attachment. This evenness [समत्वम्] of mind is called YOGA.

Recognition – that Ishwara is कर्म फल प्रदाता Karmaphalpradata" giver of fruit – result of action]" brings certain attitude. Abandoning even desire that "May Ishwara be happy with me and shower grace upon me" perform duties. And leaving longing about result keeping sameness in the facing pairs of -opposites -pain and pleasure, gain and loss, hot and cold, victory and defeat, honour and insult is called YOGA. Raaga and dwesha – result in attachment – so with the attitude of समत्वम् [sameness] raaga dweshas are neutralised. Raaga Dwesha manifest themselves through various karmas -by attitude of समत्वम्, (sameness of mind) in time – they become thinner and thinner and then become neutralised – this is what karmayoga is. Samatvam mentioned here is not with reference to actions but it is in the reference to the result of actions. Raaga dwesha can-not be overcome by just commanding yourself. Raaga dwesha constitute the person and they can't just be given up. You have to neutralise them. When actions performed with sameness – with attitude of samatvam towards result [phalam] of your karmas, they are neutralised. This attitude is KARMAYOGA. The attitude towards result of actions is called प्रसादबुद्धि ("prasad buddhi".) In Vedic culture – children are considered prasad to parents. Prasad is consecrated objects. Whatever comes from altar of Ishawara is called – Prasad. [Consecrated object] Your physical body is prasad to you as well as others. Home is prasad. The food cooked and offered to the Lord – then it is prasad. Similarly, karmaphalam is prasad. Prasadabuddhi is very important aspect of karmayoga. Therefor anything – coming – from – altar of Ishwara is prasad [consecrated object].

Vedanta indicates five types of karmas. [a] नित्य कर्म – (nitya karma) and नैमित्तिक कर्म,(naimittika karma) which can be considered together. Nitya – Karmas are karmas to be performed daily – like prayers or some rituals. These karmas depend on an individual's social status. Performing nitya karmas according to the status – whether the person is brahmachari means living a life as a student or a house holder, [a Gruhastha] a vanprasthi or a sanyasi. one gains result in the form of punya or purity of mind. Naimittik karmas are those karmas which are carried out on particular occasions, at particular time, on a particular day like on the death anniversary of – father or mother – a ritual called श्राद्ध (sraaddha,) which is to be performed monthly or on anniversary day. These karmas are done on a particular occasion – निमित्त and called naimittik karmas. Generally, naimittik karmas are performed by house holders – although sraaddha karma is done by everyone except sannyaasis. [Renunciates]. Other naimittic karmas are rituals done when the northern and southern solstices begin. Eclipses of the sun and moon.

Then there are काम्य कर्म Kamya karmas – [a ritual performed – or efforts put – purely for a given desired result.] Kamya karmas are designed and unfolded by the Vedas which tell that certain karma or ritual will produce a certain result that does not mean that kamya karmas are for antah – karana – shuddhi [purity of mind]. Many rituals are mentioned in Vedas for different desire fulfilment.

Another karmas – are called निषिद्ध कर्म-s [karmas which are prohibited karmas]– the karmas which are not to be done like हिंसा [violence]. Lying, eating meat, drinking alcohol etc.

And the karmas that are done to right a wrong कर्म is called प्रायश्चित कर्म praayashchita karmas are performed when – what is not to be done was done or there was some omission during performance of any ritual.

Thus, a particular karma can neutralise the result of wrong action – be it an omission or a commission. This praayashchita karma is effective only when the wrong – omission or commission happen by mistake not by intention

In Karmayoga – kamya karmas are given up and nitya naimittik karmas are performed as an offering to the Lord as well as for purification of mind. When you perform karma for a particular end alone you will gain only that end. You can-not gain – the prepared mind -necessary for gaining knowledge that frees you from bondages and afflictions and freedom from cycles of births and deaths. But when all karmas you perform are directed towards gaining knowledge with a prepared ready mind for knowledge through karmas – it becomes KARMAYOGA.

Any karma has four kind of results – as you have expected, more than you have expected, less then you expected and it may be totally opposite. But whatever the result is – you accept it with sameness of mind is an important aspect of karmayoga.

Without inclusion of Ishwara – there is no karmayoga. There is karmayoga only when Ishwara is understood and accepted as karma–phala–pradata– [giver of results of your actions.]

Now Sri Krishna gives the second clear definition of karmayoga.

बुद्धियुक्तो जहातीह उभे सुकृतदुष्कृते ।
तस्माद्योगाय युज्यस्व योगः कर्मसु कौशलम् ।।

**Buddhi-yukto jahātīha ubhe sukṛta-duṣkṛte;
tasmād yogāya yujyasva yogaḥ karma-su kauśalam
[BH. G. 2-50]**

Sri Krishna here says – One who has the समत्व – बुद्धि – [sameness of mind] gives up both -punyas and paapa here in this world So, commit to karmayoga. Karmayoga is discretion in action.

Take to karmayoga. Be master of your likes and dislikes [raaga and dweshas] -make yourself free from them. In this way you can be in harmony with Ishwara, certain mastery on self and enjoy inner composure. Karmayogi-s do have doer ship – unlike sannyaasi-s who don't have it. Living a life of karmayoga brings अंतः करण शुद्धि – Antah – karan – shuddhi – as it becomes free from likes and dislikes. And then आत्मज्ञानम् [Self-knowledge] is not far away.

Those who have samatvam buddhi – abandon both – punyam and paapam – and become free while living – this Samatva yoga [sameness of mind] is KAUSHALAM [DISCRETION IN ACTION]

Usually kaushalam means efficiency-perfection – actualisation. Many knowledgeable people have taken this Kaushalam as efficiency and perfection but if that is so then thieves, terrorists, cheaters – are to be considered karmayogis because their job does require quite a Kaushalam [efficiency and perfection]. Then which kind of KAUSHALAM is this? – we have to analyse.

Take any situation and you have कौशलम् KAUSHALAM of choosing action which is right – your KAUSHALAM -here what mentioned as kaushalam is this choice of action which is right in given situation. And as you have no choice over result of your action – accepting result – whatever it is with "Prasadbuddhi". When Ishawara is "Karma – phal [result] – pradata [giver]" – result may be of any kind – it is accepted without any complaint and happily – with sameness of mind is necessary and – this is the "Prasadbuddhi".

As we accept anything coming from altar of Ishwara—a pinch of ash, a spoonful of water, a small piece of fruit or sugar or may be a big laddu [sweet] full of dry fruits -we accept with same reverence and adoration, shraddha and happiness without any complaint. Similarly – Ishwara is karma – phala – pradata and result of karma comes from Ishwara – the result is prasaada and whatever it is – accept with content happily without complaint and with sameness of mind. This attitude towards result of action – whatever it is – is accepted is "Prasadbuddhi". This attitude gives a peaceful, content and happy mind which is not an ordinary thing. This – "PRASADBUDDHI" – is "KAUSHALAM"

The one without any attachment and having received – either auspicious or inauspicious – neither becomes happy nor becomes sad. Neither have likes nor dislikes – is a person with "Karma Kaushalam"

In life when one faces pairs of opposites – takes them objectively without coming into their spell while doing wherever needs to be done – this is Kaushalam.

Without inclusion of – the Ishawara – there is no karmayoga -therefore Ishwara is to be brought in life. Ishwara is to be understood – and accepted as "Karma -Phala -Pradata". Bringing Ishwara in life more and more – is Kaushalams.

Why Take to KARMAYOGA?

I need to be complete, happy, successful and I want to be immortal.

I need to have absolute satisfaction.

I need to be safe and complete. I want to live in harmony with the world.

I can't stand my incompleteness. Its experience of all that driving force behind each and every action we do and all endeavours and efforts and accomplishments don't give me the sense of being complete. This desire to have sense of being complete is natural and universal. Every human wants to be happy – uninterruptedly, secure, successful and complete. Besides no one wants to die. When these desires are natural and universal – there must be solution too. The solution is shown in Bhagvad Geeta by Sri Krishna – recommending a life style of Karmayoga.

Human birth is the best, precious and rare because in universe only human being is endowed with chance of being free from cycles of births and deaths and eternal voyage from one body to another and suffering of afflictions connected with them. At the same time human being has been given free will and given knowledge of what is right and what is wrong without being taught – therefore human being either can use this opportunity or miss it as this endowment of freedom of action – and choice can be misused also. Everyone knows what is right to do and also aware of law of Dharma. The secret of it lies in – what I expect from you – kind and right behaviour, you expect the same from me and that constitute the universal law of Dharma. Dharma is doing right in any given situation. Dharma is duty. And how karmas and duties are to be performed is shown as living a life of Karmayoga.

Mind is man. As the mind – so is individual. Mind decides your attitude, actions and personality. We meet with situations and events in life which are unpleasant and challenging. If mind is not ready and strong – with discipline, sadhana and prayerful attitude – when challenging situations have to be faced -then – that may lead to anger jealousy, frustration, regrets, shame and dissatisfaction. The weak and unhealthy mind falls "easy prey" to psycho – somatic diseases, depression and even tendency towards suicide. Geeta clearly points out action performed with right attitude – KARMAYOGA – to exhaust mental weakness and dirt. Karmayoga prepares mind to face any situation in right way -at the same time maintaining the inner content and composure.

Bhagvad Geeta is not a religious book – it is for humanity -for each and every human being – everywhere, anytime, at any age but for children and youths. Geeta is to be learnt and practised throughout life.

Geeta proclaims "BE FEARLESS" "BE NOT WEAK" and recommends KARMAYOGA – actions with right attitude – leading to clarity of mind and purity of living. The selfless activity performed in a spirit of egoless adoration and reverence to the divine would ultimately result in inner strength and purification.

Karmayogi – in time qualify for jnanam which help – having ultimate – supreme peace. Peace and happiness are synonym. This peace [Ananda – happiness] is called आत्यंतिक आनंद "Atyantic Ananda" and also called "Turiya Ananda". This Ananda [happiness] can't be compared with any other experiential Ananda as Turiya Ananda is Ananda of knowing self which is independent, natural, always with same freshness and intensity, it does not decrease with time, unlike sense produced happiness.

Karmayoga is the golden key for the supreme goal of human life.

OM

*****

Chapter 5

Moksha – Immortality

*"O the most exalted – Lord, You are revealed in the Veda-s as
"The very self in me."
May you gratify me with this intelligence.
May my body be fit – my speech be sweet.
May I listen all about you through my ears.
May I be the receptacle of Immortality.
Please, Protect all that I have heard."*

Karmayoga – in time – leads to jnanayoga. Benefits of Karmayoga are self-esteem, serenity, harmony and spiritual growth. Dedicating all actions to the Lord and accepting everything as prasad gradually lead to renounce claim of ownership and controllership, anxiety and attachments. All this increase clarity and commitment towards goal -that is moksha.

Everyone wants to live a day more happily without being ignorant. Scriptures say "You are complete, you are immortal – NOW – you need not" do" anything – for being complete and immortal.

"Am I?" naturally you utter with surprise as this looks like a statement and think how come I don't feel so? On the contrary when I compare myself with many other – objects – I found myself small, insignificant and limited. But this is because you don't know yourself – your true nature. Not only this you have judged yourself wrongly, what you consider yourself as "you" is not you – what you consider you as you is just a notion.

Now look at this. When you say "my pen" "My chair" "My car" "My son" – you know that the pen, chair, car and son are not you – they are different from you and they are objects of your knowledge. They are yours but not you. When you are asked "Who are you?" You will tell I am so and so, my name is this, I am son of so and so, I am a doctor or lawyer or teacher etc. Similarly also – you say "My legs" "My finger" "My mind" "My intellect" etc. But here you take all these things – legs, finger, mind and intellect as "I". don't you? – If you think your legs, finger, mind etc. are objects of your knowledge and so they must be different from you but you take your BMS complex as "I" because of long identification with BMS complex – births after births -because of ignorance you have taken your body as "I". Though it is known that objects of our knowledge are always different from the knower when things come to our BMS complex this mistake takes place.

Brahman

In this world there is only – "I" and "everything else" – "I" is consciousness or say Chaitanya or Atma or Brahman – one and the same and "everything else" – including BMS complex – is inert. Everything else is inert but not separate from consciousness. Consciousness [BRAHMAN] is one without another. Brahman is omnipresent. Omniscient and omnipotent. Everything is put into this Brahman. Brahman is in and through everything without being affected in any way by this everything else. Brahman is kootastha means steady – without any movement and changeless.

The word BRAHMAN is derived from Sanskrit root "BRAH". Brah means big. But how big? When you say "big ant" you know how big an ant can be. My city Rajkot is big but my state Gujarat is bigger, my state is big but the country is bigger. The country is big but the continent is bigger. The continent is big but the earth is bigger. The earth is big but the Sun is bigger. The Sun is big but still there are bigger and bigger galaxies -exist in the universe. So, BRAHMAN is how big? Brahman is limitless -scriptures say – in term of time, place and objects – BRAHMAN is limitless.

Vedanta [UPANISHADS] indicates BRAHMAN in two terms.

[a] सर्वं खलु ईदम् ब्रह्मन् । "Sarvam khalu idam BRAHMAN" All that is here is BRAHMAN or What "is" is BRAHMAN.

[B] अहम् ब्रह्मास्मि । "Aham Brahmasi" I am BRAHMAN.

As we saw earlier – "I" is BRAHMAN and everything else is inert but not separate from BRAHMAN. The

"ISNESS" is BRAHMAN. The "car is" "Pen is" "Book is" "Eye is" – in all these the "ISNESS" of car, pen, book is BRAHMAN but – "IS" is not the car, pen or book. There is a famous example of "clay pot" in VEDANTA

Understand Satya and Mithya

Take a clay pot. Now where ever you touch this pot – you touch the clay. The weight of the clay is the weight of the pot. Now on one fine day the pot said "I am sick of the clay – where ever I go it comes with me. I need space – I want to get rid of this clay" And clay said "Who wants to be with you -here I go -bye." and clay goes away. Then? Pot is also gone. Where is that pot? Pot is also gone. This pot had derived its existence from clay. If the clay is gone -the pot is also gone. The pot was clay only. But pot was there. It was useful and was holding water. What was it? That pot was a "name" and "form." It had no independent existence. It had burrowed its existent from clay only. Actually – it was not clay pot – but – potty clay. Such things which have no independent existence and depend upon something else for existence are said "MITHYA" by the scriptures.

Similarly, all objects in the universe – including your BMS COMPLEX – are nothing but mithya. They are just names and forms. They have no independent existence. They burrow their existence from BRAHMAN [consciousness] or say ATMA.

I Know "I AM"

Everyone knows that "I am" as SELF is self-effulgent. Everything is revealed in presence of Atma [the – self] only and the self is self-effulgent.

In total dark you reach home and knock the door and somebody from inside asks "Who is there?" -you will immediately say "It's me". You will not say "Come with a torch and open the door, let me see – who is here? I will see and tell you who is here." Without help of either of your sense organs or five means of knowledge you know "YOU ARE". Everyone knows clearly "I AM" without help of any means of knowledge. What is not known is – who am I. Not only this -everyone knows what the one is not. Everyone has notions – wrong conclusions about oneself that "I am small, unhappy, insignificant, nobody loves me, nobody cares for me..." and puts blames upon circumstances and from the depth of heart cries "why me?". This problem is universal – it is not personal.

Vedanta addresses to these basic problems. Vedanta states – self disapproval is wrong. There is no need for any change, any improvement for being happy and complete and teaches the self-revealing truth.

But the universal conclusion of the core person is "I am mortal" Mortal means total dissemination. Mortal is subjected to time – "I -am born" and the "Born is gone". Every born one grows old and dies. This idea of death and dissemination is disapproved.

Evidently the feelings that one is mortal, incomplete and unhappy seems to be valid. And as a short cut – human being has discovered ways to become happy by patch work. Whenever and where ever momentary, non – lasting happy moments are found – they are grabbed and go on living – and the problems of mortality, unhappiness, ignorance stay as they are. One always remains a wanting person. Therefore, the conclusion about oneself that "I am incomplete, limited, unhappy and all the endeavors to become happy and complete by changing oneself and the world may be doubted. The conclusion and the efforts are wrong. This forms the basis for the inquiry – quest to know about the true nature of the self.

Thus, the self-inquiry starts. When after achieving many accomplishments also one does not feel the sense of adequacy and completeness – then the idea that – "I am inadequate, unhappy and incomplete must be wrong." The urge to be complete and adequate is natural – there must be some solution for the same.

Everybody is Born Ignorant

Everybody is born with two -fold ignorance.

[a]   **Ignorance of the world.**
[b]   **Ignorance of oneself.**

A child is born ignorant. As it grows -it picks up knowledge, using five sense organs, memory center in the brain and experiences and – also five means of knowledge. Thus, in course the individual, nation and group of nations have piled up vast heaps of knowledge.

In relation with happiness – if I am very well informed in a particular field or many fields – if this is the knowledge – then there must be steady increase in one's – happiness too. But this is not the case.

For Knowledge of "SELF" Shraddha and Pramana [means of Knowledge]

The knowledge of the self is different from any other knowledge. "I" can-not be objectified. With objectification only you keep on shedding ignorance – and this is a continuous process and one becomes highly well – informed person. BUT "self-ignorance" persists and so all the basic problems persist. Therefore, one need not be "knowledgeable" – even if the one is highly well – informed person. I start my life with ignorance and there is no way to complete – knowledge without knowing "myself". In study of self – knowledge – subject matter is centered on "I" and "knowing" is "being" here. In all other studies "I" objectify and the knowledge and known is different from the "I".

Many discoveries are stumbled upon facts. Information can also be stumbled upon facts. The self can-not be stumbled upon. One may take many births – but self-ignorance persists unless the self is discovered and for that – individual will have to choose to know.

I know without any doubt that "I AM" but conclusion is "I am wanting, inadequate, limited" and now I want to know the true nature of myself and none of the five sense organs and also five means of knowledge are useful to me. Then how am I to know my intrinsic nature?

Means of Knowing the Self.

As the space "is", time "is", Sun "is" – the self "is". Self is not there in my perception. The words like "beauty", "intelligent" etc. are judgmental words and express esthetic appreciation. They convey some special things. For knowing self also only words are means of knowing the self. The "word mirror" of Upanishads is going to reveal the self.

The words of Veda-s which reveal the knowledge – have targeted meaning and not the words used to convey. Therefore, one can-not understand by oneself by just reading. These words are beyond one's inferences and there is no any other means to know the self. The proof of the validity of the words – is in its "self – revealing" nature. When no any other means are available – let words reveal that knowledge. For gaining knowledge an appropriate means of knowledge only is useful. Any knowledge requires two things.

[a]   It is always true to the object.

[b]   It never happens without appropriate means of knowledge.

If I want to see a form and color of a particular flower – say pink rose -I will have to employ my eyes. My nose can give me information about its fragrance but only eyes can tell me what I wanted to know. This is true for all the five senses of perception.

To know the self – then there is Upanishads [Vedanta] – and I have to look at Upanishads [scriptures] with shraddha. Shraddha is shraddha – there is no synonym for the word in any other language. Shraddha is neither trust nor faith – it is giving status to the scriptures of a means of knowledge. It is the sixth means of knowledge – PRAMANA [SHABDA PRAMANA]. To know myself I must have shraddha to what Upanishads [Bhagvad Geeta is also given a status of Upanishad] conveys and considers it as 6th means of knowledge -what's being conveyed. This means of knowledge depends on my validation. As the eyes are self-sufficient pramana – and using eye sight what the eye -sight conveys to me – I take it with shraddha, I would look at the "word mirror" of Upanishads to see what is being conveyed to me – then I conceive the words as having the status of being means of knowledge.

The nature of the knowledge of the self is such that it can be either very difficult or easy. If one is qualified in terms of -Antah – karana—Shuddhi [pure mind] – it becomes easy. The preparation for gaining qualification for this knowledge is also not that easy. The mind must be relatively free from strong likes and dislikes and should be relatively free from sorrow.

Am I – unhappy and incomplete by nature or am I just taking myself to be so? Seeking an answer to this question is a desire to know – the self. And this driving force to know may lead towards MOKSHA – which is nothing but freedom from what You don't want to have – and it is to be achieved – now -while living.

The Body of Knowledge – Vedas

There are four Veda-s
[1]   **RIGVEDA ऋग्वेद।**
[2]   SAMAVEDA – सामवेद।
[3]   YAJURVEDA यजुर्वेद।
[4]   ATHARVA VEDA. अथर्ववेद।

All the four veda-s can be classified into two sections. [1] कर्मकाण्ड Karmakand [2] Jnanakand. ज्ञानकाण्ड

All the four Veda-s present various means and ends means and for fulfilling these ends recommend certain rituals and Yajna-s. Let us see examples.

[1]   rituals for rains, Putra kameshti Yajna [sacrificial ceremonies – for progeny] Here means is unknown and end is known.

[2]   Adrashtam phalam [unknown result of any karmas] – where means is known and ends are unknown. Punyam and paapam – Good result of good karmas and bad result of bad karma – collected as "sanchit – karmas – and we don't know – how? And when? – the result of those karmas will unfold. Punya-karmas which generate good, conducive, happy situations in life and paapam – which is the result of – bad, nishidha [karmas which are prohibited by scriptures] karmas' result one has to be neutralized by experiencing painful, unconducive, difficult situations in life.

[3]   heaven and hell – where means unknown and end is also unknown

Veda-s talk about Dharma and Karma. And recommend the ways for how to get the desires fulfilled. If you want this – do this and show ways and there are three kinds of rituals as shown above. Sometimes means are known but ends are unknown, sometimes ends are unknown and means known and sometimes both are unknown but by performing what's being told to do in proper way – results are obtained surely. Veda-s also talk about do-s and don'ts. Veda-s talk about Nitya Naimittik karmas. Shows ways how to fulfil desires in dharmic way and this is a bigger section. There is one another – section for eligible – JIGNASU-S [Those who are eager to know – self] and MUMUKSHU-S [those who want MOKSHA]. This section is called – Jnanakand. The subject matter of this section is knowledge of the self [or say Brahman – Atma – Consciousness – one and the same] which is not available for any other means of knowledge and does not fall under any of the means and ends.

Everyone have wrong ideas – notions that are superimposed upon "I". One considers oneself as being man, woman, daughter, son, husband, wife, citizen, employee, employer and the variable component of the "I" confuses him/her. We all always say "I" "I" "I" but actually who this "I" is – is not known. Vedanta rightly introduces you to yourself. And on our part assimilation of the knowledge is necessary. The subject matter of Upanishads – Bhagvad Geeta is Atmajnana and it is revealed by words of Upanishads. These words make the one free from the notions that, I am – unhappy, limited, incomplete and mortal.

Atma is not BMS COMPLEX. To what I call "I" is not BMS ASSEMBLY but Atma [Brahman]. BMS complex is inert and this BMS complex is the object of your knowledge and so different from you.

Vedanta can't be put as being scientific. By itself it is means of knowledge. It is beyond the five means of knowledge. To learn Vedanta there is need of a srotriya teacher who by him/herself "knows" and – has a wholistic vision of all concepts of the scriptures. It is necessary to note at this juncture that none of the teaching Guru has claimed this knowledge – they always say that "This knowledge I have received from my teacher." And every teacher says the same thing. The original [The first guru – Adi guru] is considered to be Ishawara – Narayana or say Shivji – one and the same. Therefore, in tradition at the time of beginning of the study and beginning of every class – both – the teacher and students together chant the following verse to present their gratitude towards this "Guru shishya parampara [teacher – student tradition]

सदाशिव समारम्भं शंकराचार्य मध्यमाम् ।
अस्मदाचार्य पर्यन्तां वंदे गुरु परंपराम् ।।

Sadaashiva samaarambham shankaraachaarya madhyamaam
Asmadachaarya paryantaam vande guruparamparaam

For this knowledge – the guru paramparaa [tradition/lineage] is being remembered and offered respects.

And the Vedanta would tell – the nature of the self being non dual – SATYAM [TRUTH] and this is to be understood. There is nothing to be "GAINED," nothing to "BE". Here knowing is "being". Once known it can't be negated. This can be known by Viveki [a discriminative person]. When the absence of connection between what one wants and what one does is seen – the seer is Viveki [discriminative person]. Such discriminative person is qualified for receiving this knowledge. Such person has very clearly realized that – whatever he/she does to come out of the sense of inadequacy – leaves him/her still inadequate and limited and then the inquiry starts. Upanishads proclaim "The intrinsic nature of Atma [self] is "आनंद [Happiness]" Ananda, limitlessness, Atma, Consciousness, Brahman and Love are synonyms. What is intrinsic – is never go away till the thing is there. For example – fire's intrinsic nature is hot. Till fire exists – hotness doesn't go away. You are told "You are SAT-CHIT–ANANDA SWARUPA" [YOUR NATURE IS TRUTH – KNOWLEDGE – HAPPINESS] – YOU ARE COMPLETE AND IMMORTAL – NOW" This is difficult to believe and it looks like a statement. This is but natural as there is a long – standing delusion called "ADHYASA". This is a mistake of taking BMS COMLEX as "I". Adhyasa is described as [MISTAKE] DELUSION-MISTAKE OF TAKING BODY-MIND-SENSE COMLEX as "I" [ATMA] – The definition of अध्याय is – स्मृतिरुप: परत्र पूर्वद्रष्टावभास: ।

Smrutirupah poorvadrashtaavbhasah.

What you see is cognized in your mind – is actually not what you think it is – but you know that object – it is in your memory but you mistake the object you now seeing – taking it as the object – in your memory – which actually not that object you are seeing. Atma [consciousness] is mistaken as BMS COMPLEX. Adhyasa is superimposition. Atma is not totally unknown-is known to everyone as "I AM". If Atma is totally unknown – then it can't be locus of mistake.

If Atma is totally known then also there is no locus of mistake. Atma is evident without means of knowledge. That which requires means of knowledge is अनात्मा "Anatma" [not atma]. Here Atma is evident but ignorance prevails about nature of the Atma and therefore Adhyasa [mistake] takes place and scripture is required to remove the ignorance.

This example – Vedanta gives is very useful in understanding – this kind of mistake. You go for early morning walk in a ground where light was dim. You suddenly notice – a snake lying in front of you – it was blackish and big. You are frightened – because if you wouldn't have noticed it in time your foot would have been on the snake. You withdraw swiftly and go away. You inform – other people who were also walking on the ground. Three-four people went there to see-where the snake is lying – yes, there was a snake and one person saw it moving a bit. An another individual came on this spot and he had a torch with him – knowing the matter he threw torch light on the snake – and everyone saw that it was not a snake – it was just a rope. Everyone was relieved. Now everyone knew the snake– which was in their cognition but because of lack of proper light – they saw rope as a snake. Therefore they took the rope as a snake which was in their cognition – and this mistake took place of taking rope as snake which was not there. Snake was superimposed upon rope. Snake was not there but mistake occurred because of absence of good light and they saw the thing which was not there but it was there in their cognition. Similarly because of ignorance [dim light] – ignorance about the true nature of self and this ignorance is not total as everyone knows Atma as "I AM" and therefore superimposition of BMS COMPLEX upon Atma [consciousness] takes place. Besides – being superimposed – in reality BMS COMPLEX doesn't exists. But here – it's there – you see it, use it. You see BMS COMPLEX of all beings – how can you consider them non – existent? Scripture gives name to such things "MITHYA" which are only name and form – their existence is not independent. They burrow their existence from something else – as clay pot – which borrows it's existence from clay and pot is nothing but only a name and form – Similarly – in this world all beings' body – mind – sense assemblies – are nothing but MITHYA – totally depend upon ATMA [consciousness – the BRAHMAN] and only Atma prevails everywhere which is one without the another. And all – existence and activities can take place only in presence of ATMA [consciousness]. But ATMA is not affected by anything at all.

It is well known that two things having opposite nature do not mix. Milk and water mix to be one because both have similar nature. But if you try to mix iron pieces and milk – they will not mix – because of the opposite nature. Here the BMS COMPLEX and Consciousness [ATMA] have opposite nature but they seem mixed – the one is taken as the other. and the other is taken as the one. By mistake the one is taken as the other – and this is only possible by Adhyasa [mistake]. Ignorance denies one having knowledge of Atma. Adhyasa takes place because of ignorance – therefore – removal   of   ignorance – will reveal – knowledge of Atma. Assimilation of what's being taught by guru having wholistic knowledge of scriptures and who knows the methodology of teaching the scriptures-removes ignorance about true nature of oneself. And Adhyasa is because of superimposition of BMS COMLEX upon Atma. Atma is taken as BMS COMPLEX. "I" [Atma] as though has entered into BMS COMPLEX and so seems being limited. And as a result – this phenomenal mistake of taking body as conscious being takes place. This mistake of taking "I" as BMS COMPLEX continues till one knows his/her real intrinsic nature. Theoretical knowledge of the true nature will not serve the purpose – but the knowledge must be assimilated – [knowledge without any doubt].

Fall in Love with Yourself

Vedanta makes you fall in love with yourself. Vedanta roars "TATVAMASI" [You are THAT]. You are the cause of the world. You are SAT – CHIT-ANANDA SWARUPA. [Truth knowledge happiness is your intrinsic nature].

How is this to be assimilated? Vedanta tells "Don't believe – but – KNOW" – NOW I will have to look at scriptures with shraddha.

Atma–consciousness-brahman – Limitlessness – Love.

Atma is not BMS COMPLEX. Atma is never born – never dies. Atma is omniscient, omnipresent, omnipotent. Atma is changeless. Atma can-not be cut by any weapon nor can be made wet nor can be dried by air. What is born and dies is body. Whoever is born has to undergo six modifications.

[a]   अस्ति – Asti – comes into existence.
[b]   जायते Jayate – born.
[c]   वर्धते Vardhate – grows – to be adult.
[d]   विपरीणमते Viparinamte – undergo metamorphosis.
[e]   अपक्षियते Apakshiyate – declines.
[f]   विनश्यति। Vinashyate – dies.

These changes belong to the body. Atma doesn't take birth – so there is no question of these six modifications. Atma is always unaffected by anything. All activities become possible only in presence of Atma but Atma is not affected by any activity. This is like electricity. In a room – there is light because of electricity [through bulb or tube] – now under this light-a noble work is performed or a crime performed – electricity has nothing to do with that. Electricity just "IS". Atma is अकर्ता [non doer] and अभोक्ता [non enjoyer].

Atma is self-effulgent and all other things shine after. Everything is revealed before Atma and Atma is self-evident.

Atma is Ananda swarupa, ever existent, ever pure, all pervasive, changeless, without parts [organs] and one without another.

Once one has well ascertained – knowledge without any doubt about his/her true nature being happiness [Ananda] and wholeness – he/she remains always happy. This happiness never goes away nor it's dependent on experiences nor upon – outside objects or situation.

आत्मज्ञानी [the one who has known Atma's true nature being complete, happy and immortal] promises अभयम् [no need to fear] to all beings of the universe. None has any reason to fear from him/her. This Jnani is also fearless. Atmajnani remains same in all situations resulting in pleasure or pain because the person has known himself/ herself as ATMA [CONSCIOUSNESS] and all beings/objects and situations are not separate from ATMA is very clear to him/her. The vision of looking at all those – things take place on that view point only. Therefore, pain and pleasure become same for him/her. Atma is पूर्ण: [complete] full and – it is – the true nature of the self. Such rooted knowledge makes pain and pleasure same.

Jnani also – has to face pairs of opposites but they are, now, taken objectively while at the same time doing whatever needs to be done. Jnani looks at all the situations – including death – from view point of Atma and understands him/her self as Atma which is wholeness and so – not a single wave of reaction arises – in any circumstances. Pleasurable situation can-not increase Atma's wholeness and completeness and sorrowful situations can't decrease it. Jnani takes all kind of situations on the level of consciousness – which is full, happy, complete and any kind of situation is not capable of creating any effect here.

Atmajnani – [knower of Atma]

Bhagvan Shri KRISHNA compares jnani with the ocean in 2nd chapter of Bhagvad Geeta. As full from all sides ocean stays into its glory and remains in its place well rooted and waters from many rivers pour into it – then even – the ocean remains well rooted as it is.

In spite of added waters from rivers ocean does not get swollen – and – if waters don't come – ocean doesn't get dried. In normal circumstances – water comes or not – ocean remains same. Similarly – the Jnani knows her/his limitless nature that does not depend on any kind of situation. Whatever enters through five sense organs – in – nothing can affect or disturbs this JNANI-YOGI exactly as water comes into ocean or not – ocean remains as it is – this yogi remains same – happy and unattached – towards – flow of objects come in through five sense organs.

Now this person sees all beings into him/herself. This Jnani – now – can never perform any wrong action – as – he/she sees – self-effulgent, homogeneous Atma alone everywhere and nothing else. Does everything in the world disappears for him? No, – but everything else is mithya for this yogi. Everything is transcendented – and seen as mithya but not separate from BRAHMAN. This yogi understands that what is good for him is good for everyone.

What is Sanyasa? [Renunciation?] – and What is Immortality

Jnani is sanyasi – [renunciate] – [All sanyasis may not be jnani they may be in process but Jnani is always a sanyasi].

- Sanyasa is nothing but Atyantic Ananda [absolute happiness].
- Sanyasa is the supreme maturity.
- Sanyasa is cognitive – understanding.
- Sanyasa is ultimate peace.
- Peace and Ananda – is one and the same. Love and Ananda are also one and the same – synonyms.

This knowledge of being ATMASWARUPA makes him/her IMMORTAL while living. As – Atma – we saw earlier – neither born nor dies and BMS COMPEX is inert. And such person attains state of freedom from all afflictions, hurts and guilts, likes and dislikes and becomes free from bondages while living. His/her kartrutvam [doer-ship] and Bhoktrutvam [enjoyer-ship] go away. Therefore, now he/she seems performing actions but his/her karma account book has been closed – there is no karta [doer] – his account of karma phal registry is closed so where the results of actions are to be credited?

Therefore, in spite of performing karmas – there is no any karma phalam. But the remaining life of that yogi is like a released arrow from the bow and he/she will have to do those karmas while living remaining life and experiencing karmaphalam to get them exhausted in present life due to previous karmas because of which he/she has been born. So now in fire of jnanam all sanchit kamas [The huge amount of Adrashta phalam of karmas performed in past births] get burnt and any new karma phalam cannot be credited in the account as there is no doer ship. He/she lives with unbroken state of Ananda as there is clear understanding about the true nature of the self. When his/her body falls – the five elements of the body – Aakash, Vayu, Agni, Jalam, and earth mix with "PANCHMAHABHOOT" and he/she becomes free from cycles of birth and death. Now there is no returning. The one has attained MOKSHA while living – he/she never comes back and this state is of "Atyantic peace" [absolute peace]. And THIS IS THE IMMORTALITY.

Understanding the – Equation

Vedanta says तत्वमसि। "TAT TVAM ASI" [YOU ARE THAT]. – you are Ishawara [GOD]. "I am ISHWARA". Am I? This is not a thing which can be assimilated easily. This is an equation and equation is two sides which look different but factually is same. YOU = ISHWARA. This is – difficult to assimilate that I am the creator of this world? How? Both sides of equation are equal but it doesn't look like to be same.

In 10 = 10 there is no need for any explanation. But in 6 plus 4 = 8 plus 2 or 6 plus 4 = 100 – 90 – here the teacher will have to stress in his/her student's mind that – both sides though – evidently look different but actually it is not. Upanishad tells-" Ishwara = you" – have the evident difference but actually it is not there. To understand this equation – certain and particular preparedness is required. Here the "knowing" is "being". KNOWING is the END.

The subject matter of Upanishad-s is "ATMAJNANA" and is revealed by the words in Upanishads.

Vedanta [Upanishad-s] can-not be put as being scientific. By itself it is means of knowledge. If Veda-s say something which falls under the five means of knowledge, it is bound to be something which we already know. It is just restatement. Vedanta is अनधिगत "ANADHIGATA" means it is beyond our five means of knowledge. The words of VEDANTA have लक्ष्यार्थ "LAKSHYARTHA" [targeted meaning]. One can't employ Vedanta as a means of knowledge by oneself because then the employment is from an ignorant person. There is a need of a capable teacher who by himself or herself has a wholistic vision of all scriptures. It is important to know here – that none of the teachers has claimed this knowledge – they always say that "This knowledge I received from my teacher" and adi [first] guru [The original teacher] is considered to be the LORD NARAYANA' HIMSELF.

Therefore, the guru Parampara is saluted.

YOU ARE ATMASWARUPA AND ATMA AND ISHAWARA ARE NOT DIFFERENT.

Atma and Ishwara is one and the same – therefore ATMA is अजन्मा ajanma [never born and never die.]

And "I" am not BMS ASSEMBLY – my true nature is consciousness [BRAHMAN-ATMA – ANANDA]. When this cognition takes place – without any doubt – and as without thinking or try you know that you are a man or a woman – you know – you are atma – the Brahman– At the same time you know. "I AM IMMORTAL".

OM

*****

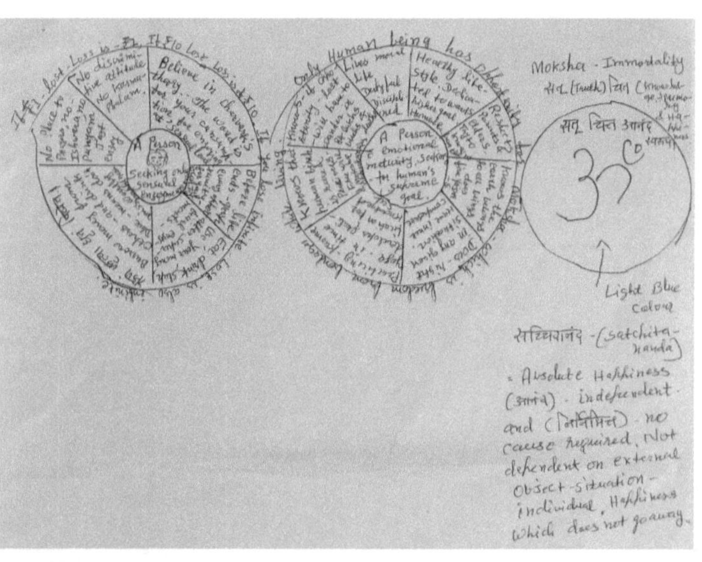

Moksha - Immortality

सच्चिदानंद - (Satchitananda)

= Absolute Happiness (आनंद) - independent. and (निर्निमित्त) - no cause required. Not dependent on external object - situation - individual. Happiness which does not go away.

Chapter 6

10 – Golden Rules of Success – from Bhagvad Geeta

Besides survival and protection – as a human being you will have to settle account with yourself. You will have to mature emotionally and have to identify and put huge efforts to neutralizes your complexes.

Messages from Bhagvad Geeta

In life when auspicious door opens because of one's lots of punya-s – the opportunity to know, to listen and to talk and discuss about Bhagvad Geeta comes. Geeta is the divine song—sung – by LORD SRI KRISHNA. Swami Vivekanand says– "Bhagvad Geeta is a beautiful bouquet of the most beautiful flowers of adhyatmic truth collected from Upanishads." Some verses are bodily lifted from the Upanishads and put there. Veda-s and Vedanta are said to be created from expiration (by using the word expiration – it is conveyed that – for the first

Guru (सदाशिव in the form of Bhagvan Dakshinamoorty) of this subtle of the all subtlest knowledge is produced so easily, so effortlessly like expiration. Watch your respiration – inspiration requires a little effort but the expiration takes place without putting effort. The PRAMANA [means of knowledge] for knowing the true nature of self-"I" – is Upanishads. Upanishads – are not product of human mind. This knowledge is given with the creation and highly intelligent – research people – scientists – RISHIS – saw this knowledge – As Newton saw the law of gravitation-which was already there – it was given with the creation – Newton "discovered" the law.

It can be asked that – is this knowledge given in Bhagvad Geeta – is relevant and useful and practical – in day-to-day life in present time? The answer is clear "YES" – because – it touches basic universal – problems of human life and shows permanent solution for them. Bhagvad Geeta gives you a road map towards success.

Everyone needs to live with harmony with the world, have self-satisfaction and need to discover self-image which is acceptable to oneself and also to the world. In spite a sense of "something lacking" – persists – even after any numbers of accomplishments.

Everyone wants to be successful and in this present time success considered– from – how many desires one can get fulfilled. Capacity to desire is – privilege and an amazing endowment.

Fulfilling desires is living a life. But discrimination in-what to desire? is important. There is a big heap of unfulfilled desires in mind. Some of the desires are fulfilled but all the desires can't be fulfilled. The unfulfilled desires make one feel defeated. And it is impossible to remain happy with so many unfulfilled desires. But in spite of so many unfulfilled desires we do feel happiness – daily in sleep, – in listening favorite music, watching smile of a sleeping child, watching glorious Sunrise etc. This proves that – it is not necessary to fulfil desires to be happy. Therefore, we need to look at this concept of success properly. The acceptability of the popular concept needs pondering. How many desires you fulfil – in all spheres – the rate of success is going to be highly fractional – therefore there is need to look at success entirely differently.

Bhagvad Geeta looks at success differently and gives redefinition of success. Success is always equal to one's self esteem. From study of Bhagvad Geeta 10 golden rules can be extracted for building one's self esteem and to be successful in life – at career front, happy family and social front also.

The 10 Golden Success Rules for Success in Life

First let us look at the rules.

[1]   Be Brave and Strong. Live a Moral Life. Be Fearless.

[2]   Live – One Day at a Time.

[3]   Do Difficult Things First.

[4]   Fake It and Make It.

[5]   Be Master of Your Senses.

[6]   Doubting Mind – Perishes – so – Act Without Doubts in Mind.

[7]   Do Karma-s [actions] That is to Be Done in Any Given Situation.

[8]   A Leading Person, Icons – Leaders – Considered to Be the Best in Any Field or Organisation and Who Are Popular Should Behave Properly as Their Speech, Behavior, Way of Living Life Affects Wide Range of People Following Them. Its Not What's Being Said, Directed or Ordered – But What They Do Have Deep Impression on Other People Working with and Following Them. So, Such People – Shreshtha – Have Great Responsibility on Their Shoulder.

[9]   Get Rid of Laziness and Idleness

[10]   Duties V/s Rights.

You may be a student, a teacher an officer, staff at any government or private offices, may be CEO of any company, a professional practicing person, business person or a parent – mother or father or home manager, you may be living/working anywhere – these 10 golden rules will put you on the royal path of success and satisfaction. Following these ten success rules will build your – high self-esteem giving you a natural sense of being a happy – and with mind free from fear.

[1] BE BRAVE AND LIVE A MORAL LIFE

Bhagvad – Geeta proclaims "Be not weak" "Be fearless" and recommends action with right attitude leading to clarity of mind and purity of living. Living a moral life in a spirit of egoless adoration and reverence to the divine – ultimately – result in inner strength and purification. You can ask – why to live purely moral life – when most of the people go for short cuts and they seem to be successful? But are they? The answer is "NO" – we saw earlier – success is always proportional to one's self esteem. So, they may seem to succeed but – not in reality. And what they lose – are very precious things without which – success doesn't mean anything.

First of all – they can't be brave and some other loss are really heavy.

[a] Prasannata [inner happiness]

They may look happy – outside – but they lack inner peace and natural happiness.

[b] They can't be fearless.

As everyone knows – what is right and what is wrong without being taught and all know about the law of Dharma – the natural inclination is always doing right in any situation but because of the pressure of binding desires they transgress boundaries of Dharma – and therefore, develop a dual personality causing restlessness in mind. Wrong doers can never be fearless. All have to face fear but the one living a moral life welcomes the fear and tells "O fear, I welcome you. I am not frightened." and does what's to be done with content mind and comes out of it.

[c] Introvert Attitude (अंतर्मुखता)

Introvert attitude gives some peace and maturity. Without peace – no one can be happy. It gives resolution of certain confusion and a clear, strong, pure mind only can give happiness. Happy state of mind is a sign of success.

[d] Mind – free from sorrow.

All have sense of being unhappy with perturbation. Their mind remains restless because of the same. Sorrowful mind can never be happy or successful.

And this loss is heavy. Conflicting emotions and double personality can't allow the person to live a life of satisfaction, peace and happiness. Though they may seem to be happy – outside – in reality – such person can't feel real happiness nor can enjoy sense of being successful. Their self-esteem gets damaged. One can hide everything from others – but one can't hide his/her intension and actions against Dharma from his/her self and this doesn't allow them to build self – esteem.

[2] SECOND RULE OF SUCCESS IS – LIVE ONE DAY AT A TIME.

Live one day at a time. Plan perfectly for one day and strictly do accordingly.

Suppose you decide to get up early in the morning for dhyana, exercise or study. You set an alarm at 4=00 am. Alarm wakes you from deep sleep – you just press the button to hush the alarm and – go to sleep again. You get up late and sincerely repent for what you did. You again swear to get up early next day and sleep. Next day morning the same thing takes place – this continues to happen often and your self-esteem gets damaged. You may take yourself as a failure and this may prevent you from a sense of being successful. Therefore, plan for one day and do accordingly – adhering to it – dedicatedly.

This may look small – but this has a – huge – impact in building your self-esteem and so in being successful.

[3] DO DIFFICULT THINGS FIRST. AND–DON'T EVER GET – FRIGHTENED

Because a thing is difficult and inconvenient – it is not to be pushed aside or postponed – and only deal with easy and convenient tasks first – such habit may prove detrimental. In – stead always deal with difficult things/tasks first and put your 100 percent – full strength and skill in – efforts.

If once you bypass doing difficult thing – slowly such incidences would go on increasing and this will make you weak, Your – strength – inside as well as outside – will decrease and it may become your habit of avoiding your difficult duties. Frequently you will avoid doing your difficult duties/tasks. These duties/tasks may be familial or may be social and also in your job – slowly decreasing your strength, your credibility and harm your self-esteem. How can such people – be successful? Some times to avoid difficult situation and imminent hard and inconvenient duties one – takes – sanyasa – which is nothing but escapism but – that way it can't be successful. Sanyasi's life style needs a well – prepared mind – otherwise to live a life style of a sanyasi is not possible.

Therefore – face the difficult things first and go through it – taking it objectively.

One must face fears also boldly. There are certain things which are worth fearing. To recognize things worth fearing is a kind of maturity. But never get frightened. Recognize fear worth fearing, welcome it and deal with it objectively.

[4] FAKE IT AND MAKE IT.

It is difficult to put in the practice – any – value-or – good habit in the beginning. – therefore – do it by putting efforts – do it intentionally. And this – in time will become natural and easy to do. Then a time comes – when you can't but follow the value and by putting efforts not to do it – you follow the value – alone – than doing anything else.

If you want to learn driving – it can be learnt by driving only. You can learn swimming by swimming only.

Two very good friends – studying together right from school – were studying now in university. Their friendship was considered an example in the campus and the friendship now – is converting slowly into love. But on one fine day – on one point – arguments took place and reached up to a bitter level. This occurred for the first time and that day for the first time they both went home separately. Both were unhappy and restless. Next day they went to university separately, attended class sitting separately, didn't speak with each other. Both – found this intensely shocking but now who will start speaking first? Both wished to talk but both had ego – in between. The boy's mother recognized from the mood of her son and asked him the reason. Knowing the reason – she advised her son to do THIS.

Accordingly, – next day, he went at the door of his friend's home with some beautiful flowers in hand and hesitantly knocked the door. His friend opened the door and was stunned seeing him standing with extended arms holding flowers in both the hands – but he was looking on left side sternly – She angrily snatched flowers from his hands and went in. The boy also left. Next day the same thing was repeated – but today both at least saw to each other. On third day – the same thing was done – and today a faint smile came on the girl's lips. On fourth day the boy – intentionally went late and his friend became restless fearing whether he will come or not? After an eager – worrisome wait when he came with flowers – the girl laughed heartily – taking flower from him and then the boy – too. What happened between them before five days was totally forgotten – the original friendly atmosphere prevailed as it was – before that fateful hour before few days.

Nothing wrong in applying "FAKE IT AND MAKE IT" method – using discrimination.

[5] BE MASTER OF YOUR SENSES.

Mind is man. Mind decides your attitude, actions and personality. In life when challenging and unpleasant situations are to be faced – then – if mind is not ready and strong with discipline, sadhana and prayerful attitude it may lead to anger, jealousy, regrets, frustration, dissatisfaction. The weak and unhealthy mind falls "easy prey" to psycho somatic diseases, depression and even tendency towards suicide. Ask any Psychologist – how many patients of Depression they deal with? And more developed the country – more the cases – and the rate of suicides is also high. These all happens because of "wrong value – based" society. Today the central value is money and false definition of success. Were there central – "DUTY" – and were all performing their duties properly – according to their roles – there would have prevailed satisfaction and self – esteem solving so many psychological problems. To value – values is very important.

One must not be carried away on ride by their senses and internal enemies like obsessive desires, anger, delusion, ego, jealousy and greed.

In Kathopanishad's 3rd valli's – 3rd verse – an analogy is presented beautifully. Human body is compared with a chariot. Imagine a chariot – with five horses, a charioteer with reigns in his hands with which he/she controls – the horses. And there are roads on which these horses are running and a rear seat behind the seat of charioteer – where sits the master of the chariot. Now here – the pure discriminating intellect is compared with the charioteer. The – reigns is the mind – with which the intellect [The charioteer] controls the movements of the(horses) body. The horses [and the instincts] are the five sense – organs – and the roads are the sense objects.

Senses [horses] naturally report about objects of their respective fields [Eyes reports objects coming in the field of their vision, ears report – sounds, nose reports about smell, tongue reports about taste and skin reports about touch. The sense – organs are just reporters.] and attraction of these objects pulls body to enjoy those objects. Intellect is charioteer. Our intellect takes decision and these decisions decide our path in life. Discrimination and lack of discrimination – both are there in our intellect. When – ever decision is to be taken – intellect only takes it – and accordingly our life shapes up – therefore intellect is compared with charioteer. The reigns of the horses is mind which is – in the hands of the charioteer – [The mind is in control of the – intellect]. By reigns the charioteer controls the horses – the senses. [the intellect controls the senses through mind].

Undisciplined and untrained mind sometimes becomes so strong and non-cooperative that – the decision taken by intellect can't be applied. If reigns [mind] are loose – and horses – [senses] – can-not be controlled by intellect because of undisciplined – non co-operative mind – and so the senses behave as they wish. All the five horses may try to run on different roads and mind being weak and unruly – intellect can't control the horses then the chariot is bound to fall apart and get destroyed.

The master of the chariot is – Atma [self] – but here it is not to be taken as pure consciousness but it is jiva– soul the subtle body which identifies with the mind and intellect. [Atma is neither doer nor enjoyer] – this we have seen earlier].

This world has capacity to give you some happiness and– certain accomplishments – but if the mind is not disciplined, strong and prepared – one can get only bumpy life -then where is the question of happy, successful, secure and complete life?

Therefore, Sri Krishna talks about – व्यावसायात्मिका बुद्धि (vyavasayika buddhi-) capacity to certain assimilation. And who have vyavasayika buddhi – can see that there is no connection between what they want and what they do. Mind which is not your friend will go on various paths and will not be able to concentrate on the path which has been chosen. The mind that is not together goes to many directions and the person can't know with clarity about the goal and can't develop the attributes needed for gaining success. Therefore, intellect must be strong enough to control mind and to make mind – control senses by readjusting, tightening the reigns so that the horses [senses] are made to go on right path and do not cause destruction. You must not be carried away on ride by your senses and internal enemies – like kama – [obsessive desires], anger, moha [delusion], ego, jealousy and greed. There is nothing wrong – in achieving power, being highly knowledgeable and earning money – Vedanta – in Karmakand section shows – how to achieve such things. But with power-sympathy and justice, with knowledge – humbleness and with wealth [richness – being wealthy in terms of money] magnanimousness/ generosity must go together – otherwise the same attributes can become cause of destruction of themselves and others. Therefore, to make mind friend, worthy and well trained is necessary.

To make your mind – your-best-friend – you should have – four kind of attributes– which are present in every one in more or less degree – but these four attributes must be made very well rooted in mind. These attributes give you pure mind that gives you clarity and qualification to achieve the supreme goal in life.

These attributes are...

[1] VIVEKA [DISCRIMINATION]

Knowledge of – what is नित्य nitya [ever existent] and what is अनित्य – anitya [perishable].

You want continuous – permanent happiness and completeness – for which – you depend on anitya objects – the result is bound to be perishable. So it is important to know what is nitya – what is anitya. [What is perishable and what is non-perishable.]

[2] DISPASSION [VAIRAGYA]

This is absence of attachment. Abandoning everything. This doesn't mean – abandoning loving and meaningful relationships and use of any comforting or luxurious things nor it is dislike and hate for them nor it is putting them away – fearfully but it is ending dependency on them. Vairagya [tendency towards dispassion] is growing over those things. Vairagya is neither impulse nor dislike – it is understanding. It is seeing things objectively.

[3] SHAT -SAMPATTI [A GROUP OF SIX ATTRIBUTES WHICH IS LIKE A WEALTH]

[A] शम: | SHAMAH

This is control over mind-control over impulsive desires at intellect level. By controlling mind – keeping reigns tight – not allowing horses [senses] any unruly behavior- you become real master. Control over mind called "MANONIGRAH" – is not an ordinary thing.

[B] दम: – DAMAH –

Restraint at the level of senses is Damah. This is not denial without understanding. This is restraint with understanding and it is to be practiced with SHAMAH -only. You are the one who decides your boundaries if you want to – achieve your goal, happiness and security. You should enjoy and consume things as much as you need for maintaining your health and peace of mind – and that's Shamah and Damah. If you live in this way – then your whole life is penance only.

[C] उपरम – *UPARAMAH*

It is following your Dharma [duties] with steadfast attitude. If you are living a life of Shamah and Damah – in time – UPARAMAH takes place automatically. Then you follow naturally – your Damah without putting any efforts. Your duties may not be easy but you feel joy if you perform – all your duties alone. And, think, if everyone performs duties like that – there will never be any discordant note in the music orchestra of harmony.

When we learn cycling – in the beginning it becomes difficult to maintain balance – we fall many a times – bruising our knees. But once we learn thoroughly – we can ride a cycle – without holding its governor – at the same time singing a song and whistling. Practicing Shamah and Damah makes – Uparam – equally easy – like – cycling – without holding the governor and at the same time whistling.

[D] *TITIKSHA SAMENESS OF MIND IN FACING PAIRS OF OPPOSITES*

Sameness of mind in facing – hot and cold – at the level of body, happiness and unhappiness -at the level of mind, – honor and insult at the level of intellect. In everyone's life – at one stage and time some of the pairs of opposites are bound to be faced. In lack of titiksha – the mind is not ready and strong enough – it becomes difficult to face such situations with maintaining inner composure and the one becomes victim of anger, jealousy, frustration, regrets, shame and suffer psycho somatic diseases, depression and also may be drawn to commit suicide. Therefore, – training mind with titiksha – sameness of mind [samatvam] is necessary. This attribute you will have to develop. In facing the pairs of opposites and in moments of happiness and unhappiness – your mind should remain relatively same. You will have to develop enough strength to tolerate– body, mind and intellect related inconvenience -because outside attacks can-not be avoided but – you can adjust and manage your internal reaction. In absence of reaction the attack becomes without any impact and effect. Once you have Titiksha – then when such attack takes place – you can do whatever is needed to be done – with contented mind and without worry. There is nothing wrong if you apply ways to decrease hot or cold -but you should not be restless and complaining – while facing those situations in absence of facilities of the means-to decrease the intensity of those attacks.

To have mind without complaint – is a great – blessings.

Remember that famous and beautiful PRARTHANA?

"O Ishwara, may I have the maturity to accept totally – gracefully, what I can-not change, the will and effort to change what I can and the knowledge of the difference between what I can and can-not change"

It is likes and dislikes [Raaga and Dwesha] only which are the cause of restless – peaceless mind.

[E] श्रद्धा – *SHRADDHA – SHRADDHA IS SHRADDHA IS SHRADDHA. –*

There is no synonym of the word "Shraddha" in any language.

To gain any knowledge – shraddha is necessary. If we wish to learn anything and – we are totally – ignorant about – we must have shraddha on the person who is going to give that knowledge. It may look – sometimes – that sayings/ teaching – is opposite -at that time lack of shraddha should not arise but the thing must be kept on pending inquiry. There is absence of knowledge and the one who has the knowledge is being subjected to ashraddha then where is the chance of knowledge taking place?

Shraddha is defined by the scriptures as giving the status of being means of – knowledge – "shabda pramana" [words as means of knowledge.] If status of being pramana is not given to the words of Upanishads – then knowledge can-not take place. The scriptures can-not be understood by just reading because there are so many technological words, one word can be used for many different meanings and what's the meaning of the word is to be taken as per context. There is a special methodology of teaching and for that a capable srotriya teacher who has wholistic knowledge of – scriptures – that only can teach.

To have shraddha is very special grace of Ishwara. By – efforts one can't gain this knowledge – oneself.

[F] समाधान–चित्तनैश्चल्यम् *-SAMADHANA–CHIT- NAISHCHALYAM*

Full attention and concentration on – one thing alone in mind. The mind keeps – on top priority and constantly with firm determination to achieve the determined goal – is SAMADHAN. The center behind all activities is only in that one goal is SAMADHANA.

Enjoining all the strength in achieving that goal is SAMADHANA.

One student decides to super-specialize in one particular medical field – and then his/her each action is aimed to achieve that goal – he/she will eat nutritious and just enough meals – to avoid sleepiness or exercise or watch TV or a film to get fresh his mind – entire activities he/she performs are aimed to attain that decided goal. All activities that are helpful in achieving the goal alone are performed. If there is commitment towards the goal then control over senses and abandonment over activities harmful in reaching up to the goal will take place automatically.

[4] मुमुक्षुत्वम् *MUMUKSHUTVAM – "MAY I ATTAIN MOKSHA".*

Moksha means freedom – to get free. And to have this desire is sign of maturity;

What is this desire for freedom is? To understand this one will have to know – what is bondage. Knowing what is bondage – desire takes place to be free from that bondage is necessary.

Bondage means dependency -depending on other outside objects for happiness, security. Completeness. In life one has to face different kinds of dependencies as pertaining to body, job, -relations etc. And if none of them – then even everyone has sense of lacking something in every situation. By fulfilling desires -this feeling of lacking is tried to be solved – then even one never feels being – complete. This sense of "lacking something" -is bondage. The biggest bondage is cycles of births and deaths. Desire to be free from these bondages is MUMUKSHUTVAM.

Absence of sense of -being unhappy, incomplete and insecure is MOKSHA. The world – will never behave according to our wish. Let the world run as it is – but develop an art of remaining – untouched – unaffected by the world's behavior -is an art of living and that frees you from the bondages.

Everyone – including the one who perform activities for -Artha – kama [for happiness and security -depending up on perishable – [anitya objects] and activities to fulfill desires – is also performed for MOKSHA alone. Because they also want to be free from the sense of limitation -and for that purpose only perform these activities. Only they are finding the freedom where there is no any possibility that they can fulfil the same.

When the desire for MOKSHA becomes exactly like – suffocation you experience when your head is under water and someone holding you down – not allowing you outside -over the surface of water of a river – then that desire of coming out and breathe in air – similar desire for Moksha is called MUMUKSHUTVAM – [desiring moksha.]ss

[6] संशयात्मा विनश्यति। SANSHAYATMAA VINASHYATI DOULTING MIND PERISHES

अज्ञश्चाश्रद्दधानश्च संशयात्मा विनश्यति ।
नायं लोकोऽस्ति न परो न सुखं संशयात्मनः।।

**Ajñaś cāśraddadhānaś ca samśayātmā vinaśyati;
nāyam loko'sti na paro na sukham samśayātmanaḥ.
[BH. G. 4-40]**

The one without discrimination and faith and having doubting mind – perishes. Doubting one can accomplish nothing in this world -nothing the world beyond – nor the one can be happy.

There are two types of doubts.—
[a]   About one's own capabilities.
[b]   Doubt about success in action undertaken. Here we must refer this important verse.

उद्यमं साहसं धैर्यं बुद्धि: शक्ति: पराक्रम: ।
षडेते यत्र वर्तन्ते तंत्र दैव सहायकृत ।।

**Udyamam saahasam dhiryam buddhih shaktih
paraakramh
Shadete yatra vartante tatra daiva sahaykruta.**

उद्यमम्।

Udyamam – Cntinuously working over the task/ undertaken work – is udyama.

साहसम्।

Sahasam – If need arises – readiness to take risky steps and learning new things and apply to the task undertaken.

धैर्यम्।

Dhairyam – This is not only performing action calmly. But it is – performing the undertaken task till – the desired result obtains.

बुद्धि:।

Buddhi-hi – is the decision taking capacity – in alignment of need – with understanding and balance and when necessary – capacity of taking instant decision

शक्ति:।

Shakti-hi – This is capacity to handle all aspects of the task undertaken and actualization in performing it.

पराक्रम: |

Parakrama-h -When difficulties, hurdles come – these challenges are faced with courage, tackled with content and proceed further, that's parakram.

In second line of this verse – it is said that – LUCK – helps only -where these six attributes prevail.

In spite of having all the required attributes – and putting -100 per cent efforts – result may not come as expected -because of "DAIVAM" [LUCK] which is nothing but result of our own past actions. Our choice is in performing actions but once performed – we don't have any choice over the results. Karma Phala -Pradata [giver of results of our actions] is ISHWARA. When? Where? And how? Is not known. We will have to exhaust the karma by experiencing its phalam [result – which may be either pleasant or painful] – is no one knows.

When you need help then seek help – and you must seek help from omniscient, omni potent, omnipresent – sarvashakte-h – [ISHWARA]. You can ask – "Then what about purusharth [human efforts]? They are not opposite each other. Prarthana [prayers] is also a karma with its inbuilt results -which will depend how sincerely, with how much absorption and with which intensity – the one connects with Ishwara.

Grace of Ishwara is falling everywhere and upon all beings – one will have to tap it. As Sun rays' are present everywhere but to have them you must open the window.

Therefore undertaking any task – put 100 per cent efforts and resources without – doubting own capabilities and without over thinking about the result.

The doubting self goes to destruction.

Self – doubt is detrimental to oneself.

Again – here appears KARMAYOGA. Sameness of mind and PRASADBUDDHI attitude towards result of any action is buddhiyoga.

[7]   NIYATAM KURU KARMANI – PERFORM NIYATA [SHASHTRA RECOMMENDED KARMAS THAT IS TO BE DONE] KARMA-S [ACTIONS]

नियतं कुरु कर्म त्वं कर्म ज्यायो ह्यकर्मणः।
शरीरयात्रापि च ते न प्रसिद्ध्येदकर्मणः।।

Niyataṁ kuru karma tvaṁ karma jyāyo hyakarmaṇaḥ;
śarīra-yātrā'pi ca te na prasiddhyed akarmaṇaḥ.
[BH. G. 3-8]

Do karma that is to be done – because action is superior to inaction. The ideal form of karmayoga is Nitya – karma. NITYA KARMA OR VIHIT KARMA are actions which are to be performed daily. The five yajnas – we saw earlier [Brahma yajna, deva yajna, Pitru yajna, Bhoot Yajna and Nru Yajna] are nitya karmas. Then daily routine like bath, daily worship, preparing food with thinking that -this food is being prepared for your home pooja – prasthapit Ishtadeva, chanting mantras and teaching certain mantras and values from scriptures to the children of the home – to contribute in maintaining the chain of this knowledge as it has been maintained and brought up to you by efforts of your ancestors – it's your duty that now you hand over the same to the next generation. Performing – nitya karma – results into Antah Karana – Shuddhi.

Nitya karma also includes one's duties. They are.
[1]   Universal duties – common for all.
[2]   Vishesh duties. [Particular duties – according to the role] – to be performed according to roles, time, place and situation.

Universal values are to be followed for harmony of the universe and all know about these – duties without being taught.

Vishesh duties are – according to your roles and you perform many roles. Whatever role you perform you need to do what is to be done – in the given situation – and that becomes your "SWAKARMA" i.e. -What is to be done in that role – in given situation. Your SWAKARMA is – "ARCHANA" [OFFERING] unto the Ishwara.

At the same time – remember – you should give "quality time" [a time when no TV, no radio, no news – paper, no phone] to your children and spouse and parents. This also is your swakarma. This contributes a lot in your satisfaction and happiness.

[8] परिहार्य and अपरिहार्य। PARIHARYA AND APARIHARYA [AND DIFFICULT THING FIRST] -SITUATIONS. KNOW AND ACCEPT BOTH.

[A] परिहार्य -Pariharya – is a situation in which you can do something to restore, to repair, to regain – what is being lost -the situations – which have remedy – something is possible to do for the loss. Certain situations are अपरिहार्य "Apariharya" – that means – nothing can be done about that. The loss is for ever -can't – be fulfilled.

As an example -in tsunami -all objects in home – furniture etc. get drowned away. The loss is big but it is PARIHARYA. You can restore them – may be that's difficult, takes some time. But the house can be again be arranged with necessary furniture, beddings, kitchen facilities etc. BUT when family members drowned away and died – this is "APARIHARYA" situation. This loss can-not be fulfilled.

These two things are to be understood and accepted clearly.

We have to accept -what is Apariharya. Sooner the later – because if you remain in deep sorrow – you can't progress, can't accomplish anything. There are so many possibilities in life but deep sorrow does not keep anyone capable to do or achieve anything to progress in life. And the precious human life goes in vain. This neither helps the one, nor to others – therefore the distance between "what?"......to... "so what?" must decrease.

For – gaining the – "so what?" position acceptance has an important role.

For offices and organizations -non-acceptance of laziness and idleness is very important – sooner getting rid of that – the better.

The two – laziness and idleness – are different. Laziness is starting problem. Idleness is one looks active but nothing accomplished.

And third problem is postponement of difficult things. Finding thing difficult – it is postponed – if once that thing postponed – then two things happen.

The inner strength will decrease – making you a bit weak. Secondly – slowly – habit of putting aside – even less difficult things will develop. More and more things will be kept pending and postponed for their solution. On individual level such people lose their inner strength, besides what they lose is self – esteem.

The organization, office or institution get affected with such tendencies – losing their credibility. Therefore. Laziness and idleness and also habit of postponing difficult things are not to be allowed.

Similar idleness is a confused tendency towards and procrastination.'

These will result in poor outcome – and slowly the efficiency and reputation get affected.

In your office/organization – such people -are to be sacrificed. But – then even try to help the person – some other way – certain things you just can-not allow to practice.

यद्यदाचरति श्रेष्ठस्तत्तदेवेतरो जनः।
स यत्प्रमाणं कुरुते लोकस्तदनुवर्तते ।।

Yad yad ācarati śreṣṭhas tat tad evetaro janaḥ;
sa yat pramāṇaṁ kurute lokas tad anuvartate.
[BH. G. 3-21]

Whatever an important person does that alone the other people do. Whatever that person sets as proper, the world of people follows.

Whatever – an important person does, that the other people do – imitate. Whatever he/she sets up as the standard that – the people under their influence follow.

So being a leading person, a person who widely interacting with people, who is head of any institution, organization, hostels, hospitals, companies, family, icons in various fields like sports, acting, music – all are to be considered "SHRESHTHAH". It is not their advice – not their orders – nor – instruction but only their conduct which will have impact on the people. Similarly, children will observe their parents' behavior and they just ignore their advice – but there will be permanent impact on their mind of how they behave. This impression shapes their adulthood. If you can give your children high head – because of honesty, hard work and truth – "rutam" that is alignment in thinking – speaking and doing – it is a great legacy -you are handing over. By doing this you are in harmony with your family – not only this but you are also – in harmony with society, country and the world and universe also.

So whoever is – "SHRESHTHAH" -have great responsibility and they must look after the level – the standard of their speech and behavior, their style of wearing dignified dress, style and habits of eating and drinking. If these icons' behavior is not proper – their fans' behavior also will not be proper. And lives of many influenced youths and people's lives go wrong way -causing them big loss.

For this reason alone – it is observed that in any institution or organization with the change of the head – the work culture changes drastically – either for good or for bad.

Therefore – in creating a healthy, strong, disciplined and dutiful society – such shreshtha have important role and responsibility. Everyone must be alert in choosing their "SHRESHTHAH" – because wrong choice can destroy them. And if you are "SHRESHTHAH" you must be very vigilant about your life style.

One another point which looks small but having huge impact is – use of words like "thanks" and "sorry", "nice" "wonderful" etc. We use these words often and repeatedly. It's nice to use those words. Nothing wrong – only – when – you say "Thanks' 'or "sorry" don't utter the words only for sake of saying – but feel in the same way. If you say 'wonderful" feel wonderful. When say 'thanks" feel thankful. Do this and feel the difference.

And last but not the list – here is the 10th success rule – it is...

[10] कर्तव्य और हक्क।

Duties V/s. Rights

Animals, insects, trees, birds – are programmed unlike human being. Therefore, human beings have to handle…

[a]   Survival – which is common – like animal kingdom.

[b]   Protection – again like animals-birds etc.

AND

[c]   Unlike animal kingdom – human will have to settle account with – self. Because being self-consciousness – human being has judgement about him/her self and also for the world and as a result have complexes. The free will and desire – of improvement – to be better and different -which come from self-consciousness has an element of pressure which comes from complete self – consciousness and judgement – resulting in complexes and therefore problems too. Animals don't have complexes and so no problems, too. It requires a great effort and maturity to grow out of one's complexes.

Swakarma [One's own duties] helps a lot.

श्रेयान्स्वधर्मो विगुण:परधर्मात्स्वनुष्ठितात् ।
स्वधर्मे निधनं श्रेय:परधर्मो भयावहः ॥

Śreyān sva-dharmo viguṇaḥ para-dharmāt svanuṣṭhitāt;
sva-dharme nidhanaṁ śreyaḥ para-dharmo bhayāvahaḥ.

[BH. G. 3-35]

One's own imperfectly performed "Dharma" is better than the well performed "Dharma" of another. Death in one's own "Dharma" is better. The "Dharma" of another is fraught with fear.

Dharma is duties.

The spirit behind the concept of duty is still valid. While changing jobs and duties of roles become when the aim is only money.

Yogastha kuru karmaani sangama tyaktvaa dhananjaya
Siddhyasiddhyoh samo bhutvaa Samatvam Yoga Uchyate
[BH. G. 2-48]

Perform action abandoning attachment, being steadfast in "yoga" and balanced in success and failures. Evenness of mind is called YOGA.

There are two types of Dharma – remember – dharma means duties.

[a]   Common Dharma.

[b]   Vishesh [particular duties assigned to the role you are playing] Dharma.

Common dharma is universal. The base of this dharma is -in "what you expect from me – I expect same from you". And therefore, everyone knows what is dharma – without being taught. The law is given with the creation. Such laws can-not be disobeyed, – if disobey – you have to suffer. These laws operate infallibly and impartially.

The definition of dharma is simple – "To do what is to be done [what is right is done] in – any given situation, time and place" is Dharma and to do what is to be done with proper attitude is KARMAYOGA.

Now you play so many roles which go on changing. You are talking with your father – you are playing a role of a son – at the same time your son enters and starts telling you something happened in his school -now you are a father – now your wife comes and asks you to do something – and you are a husband. Every role you are playing has a script which go on changing as per your role and your relationship. So, you have different script – duties -responsibilities as a son, father, mother, husband, wife employer, employee, citizen etc.

There are two things-you have-duties and also you have rights. Because of the total self-consciousness you have judgement about yourself and also for the others -also for the world too. And the basic problem of human being is notions about him/her/itself that " I am unhappy, limited and incomplete" I am lacking something" and "why me?" and then for this – circumstances and some near and dear – blamed. One also feels – that he/she did so much for them but they have not appreciated or even taken any notice of his/her sacrifices and efforts for helping them.

Because the central value is something else and not "DUTY" and faulty understanding about what success is – this happens. A healthy society can exists if the society is built on a value – "duty first". The central value is performing duties in any circumstances – builds a heathy, happy, strong and prosperous society – because one performs his/her duties and the other enjoys his/her rights. If son performs his duties – it becomes the rights of his parents. Parents doing their duties – and -son/daughter enjoy their rights. Similarly, by performing respective duties -husband and wife enjoy their rights. This goes with each role and if duties – whether hard or easy, convenient or not and demanding sacrifices or not – every one performs duties – both universal and Vishesha – then everyone 's rights are being taken care – automatically and harmony prevails.

Therefore, duties are not opposite of rights -but they go together.

You grow performing your duties alone, may your duties be small and insignificant or difficult and challenging – perform – because it's your duties.

Human birth is meant for growing. By growing you become successful. Thus by redefining – definition of success – YOU – SOON KNOW THAT YOU ARE THE CONQUEROR

YOU ARE THE CONQUEROR

OM...OM...OM

*****

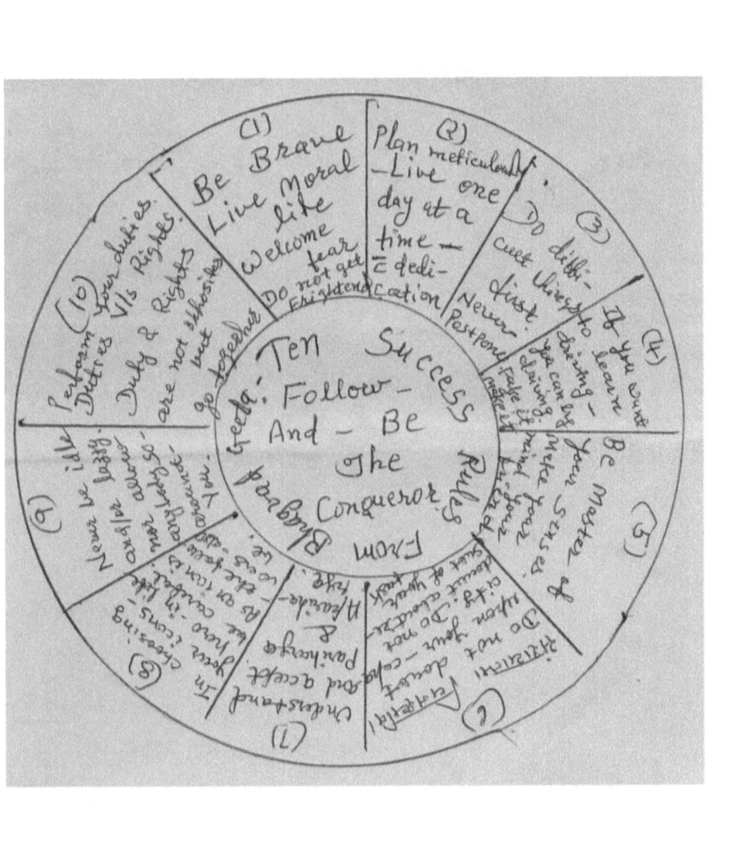

Ten Success Rules
From Bhagwad Geeta.
Follow - And - Be The Conqueror.
(1) Be Brave Live Moral life Welcome fear Do not get Frightened
(2) Plan meticulously - Live one day at a time - & dedication
(3) Do difficult things to learn first. Never Postpone
(4) If you want to learn - Be Master of your senses
(5)
(6)
(7) Understand and accept Partnership
(8) In choosing your actions
(9) Never be lazy
(10) Perform Your duties. Duties V/s Rights. Duty & Rights are not otherwise but go together

9 798889 544529